Advance Acclaim

"*Teaching to Every Kid's Potential* is not a dreaded 'flavor of the year' educational reform. Instead, the approach in this book is to slightly tweak what we do every day—in the classroom, out on the playground, on the favorite end-of-the-year field trip—to connect with and spark the fire of learning in each student. Layne Kalbfleisch has shared with us invaluable neuroscience research on learning, great insight about its practical application and, most importantly, the belief that *all* children can learn, and that we are capable of providing the enriched environment to *enable* all children to learn. This is a must-read for every student teacher, teacher, school administrator, and university education professor!"

—**Vannetta R. Perry, Ed.D.,** Former Superintendent of Schools,
Magdalena, New Mexico

"The opening chapter of *Teaching to Every Kid's Potential* contains a sentence which is both a statement of fact and a call to action: 'We haven't yet achieved the rapport to really marry the fields of education and neuroscience.' Written by someone who is both an accomplished cognitive neuroscientist and a seasoned hands-on educator, this book goes a long way toward accomplishing that rapport. In a concise and accessible manner, Layne Kalbfleisch places some of the central concepts of cognitive neuroscience in a direct educational context."

—**Elkhonon Goldberg, Ph.D.,** Director, Luria Neuroscience
Institute, and Clinical Professor of Neurology, Grossman
NYU School of Medicine

"One of the greatest challenges facing scholars such as Dr. Kalbfleisch is to connect neuroscientific research and concepts to real world applications. This excellent book builds the bridge and points the way to future possibilities."

—**Jack A. Naglieri, Ph.D.,** Research Professor, University of
Virginia, Emeritus Professor George Mason University and
Senior Research Scientist, Devereux Center for
Resilient Children

T0339198

"This is a remarkable book. It is an essay on what I imagine as an emerging double helix of education best practices and evolving neuroscience. The author, an educational psychologist, challenges many current educational sacred cows and offers creative, imaginative, emotionally-informed, and science-based alternatives. Kalbfleisch offers to educators of all types a vision of the world in which teachers and students are not inanimate stick figures or electronic data storage silos for uploading and downloading. Her 'four imperatives'—flexibility, readiness, connection, and (un)masking—provide the cognitive/affective/relational architecture to help realize 'every kid's potential' (to which I add: 'and every teacher's potential as well')."

—**Howard F. Stein,** Professor Emeritus in the Department of Family and Preventive Medicine, University of Oklahoma Health Sciences Center

TEACHING TO EVERY KID'S POTENTIAL

TEACHING TO EVERY KID'S POTENTIAL

Simple NEUROSCIENCE LESSONS to Liberate Learners

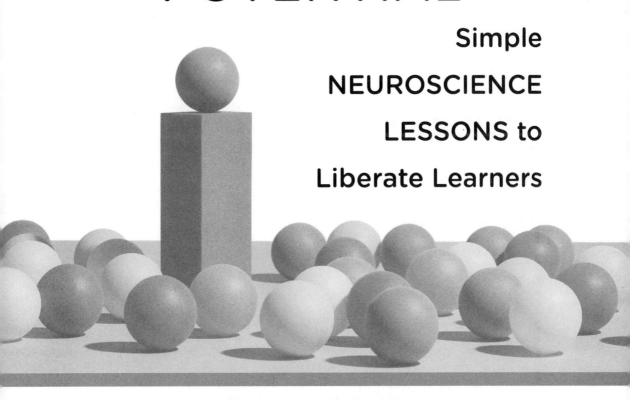

LAYNE KALBFLEISCH

W. W. NORTON & COMPANY

Independent Publishers Since 1923

Note to Readers: This work is intended as a general information resource for teachers and school administrators. Models and/or techniques described are illustrative or are included for general informational purposes only. Neither the publisher nor the author can guarantee the efficacy or appropriateness of any particular recommendation in every circumstance. For case-specific questions and guidance, please consult with your school and/or community mental-health clinicians. The names of all students mentioned have been changed and identifying details changed or omitted. Any URLs displayed in this book link or refer to websites that existed as of press time. The publisher is not responsible for, and should not be deemed to endorse or recommend, any website other than its own or any content not created by it. The author, likewise, is not responsible for any third-party material.

For information about permission to reproduce selections from this book, write to Permissions, W. W. Norton & Company, Inc., 500 Fifth Avenue, New York, NY 10110

For information about special discounts for bulk purchases, please contact W. W. Norton Special Sales at specialsales@wwnorton.com or 800-233-4830

Manufacturing by Sheridan Books
Production manager: Katelyn MacKenzie

Library of Congress Cataloging-in-Publication Data

Names: Kalbfleisch, M. Layne, author.
Title: Teaching to every kid's potential : simple neuroscience lessons to
   liberate learners / Layne Kalbfleisch.
Description: First edition. | New York, NY ; London : W.W. Norton &
   Company, 2021. | Series: Norton books in education | Includes
   bibliographical references.
Identifiers: LCCN 2020047540 | ISBN 9780393713084 (paperback) | ISBN
   9780393713091 (epub)
Subjects: LCSH: Individualized instruction. | Classroom environment. |
   Cognitive neuroscience. | Academic achievement--Psychological aspects.
Classification: LCC LB1031 .K34 2021 | DDC 371.39/4--dc23
LC record available at https://lccn.loc.gov/2020047540

W. W. Norton & Company, Inc., 500 Fifth Avenue, New York, N.Y. 10110
www.wwnorton.com

W. W. Norton & Company Ltd., 15 Carlisle Street, London W1D 3BS

1 2 3 4 5 6 7 8 9 0

Contents

Acknowledgments

Bringing this book to maturity took three years, two editors, and one author! My gratitude goes to my editor, Carol Collins, and her team, Mariah Eppes and Jamie Vincent, for their patience, sharp eye for detail, and good cheer.

How do we teach so that knowledge transfers and how do we transfer knowledge between neuroscience and education about those processes so that we can teach and learn better? The four neurological imperatives you will encounter for learning, one in each chapter, are the result of a lot of thinking about that. I can see clearly the children and young adults whose learning opportunities will change for the better because we're going to improve at recognizing them and learning with them. The children in my life, from my practice, and especially my grandchildren, nieces, and nephew, whose needs, curiosity about the world, talent, and thirst for knowledge, mirror back to me what you will encounter in this book.

Thank you to my students at Northern New Mexico College, and to young master Fermin, my "consultant." Thank you to my husband, family, and dear friends who have lived with my activities and preoccupation in service of "the book." I dedicate it to all of you and to current and future teachers and learners as we adapt to pandemic constraints and opportunities; thriving and learning anew. Thank you. I'm so grateful. Miigwech.

Layne Kalbfleisch
December 14th, 2020

Introduction

Education needs some new behavioral policies that will bring instruction in line with our human neurology and support the inevitable and ever-present individual differences in how people learn. By "behavioral policies" I mean that there are certain assumptions made during teaching and learning that we now know are not in line with how we are neurologically wired. These are neurological imperatives emerging from cognitive neuroscience that suggest new directions for teaching and learning and how we school. This book is about the fruitful crossings and intersections materializing from the learning sciences today.

Even though education neuroscience is in its infancy and many of the studies with humans are only mature at the correlational level, there are markers and indicators emerging that suggest how we might adjust teaching to better match how humans really function. Students give teachers plenty of evidence every day that our current system isn't working. Neuroscience offers a blueprint for human learning, a set of principles we can follow that align with our neurology instead of competing with it or working against it.

We need a common vocabulary and a set of concepts to understand what it is we are really seeing when students are off task, disinterested, struggling, and not working to potential. More importantly, we're not seeing their potential when it is right in front of us. I hope this book will help change that by showing how you can:

- befriend distraction, see it for the asset it really is in the learning process, and capitalize on it strategically to promote cognitive flexibility;
- set learning conditions to stabilize and promote safety, well-being, and higher level thinking;
- deepen the role you play in influencing the quality of the learning that happens on your watch, through teamwork and collaboration;
- recognize the behaviors of executive function and how skills, abilities, and precise weaknesses mask our opportunity to see the roots of those behaviors; and
- find a simpler way to identify and address behaviors that stymie your best plans.

Who Is This Book For?

This book is for anyone who teaches, whether outdoors, in a classroom, museum, library, art studio, or the workplace. It is also for anyone curious about the learning sciences—a field that incorporates pedagogical design, curriculum development, child development, brain development, educational psychology, special education, cognitive neuroscience, medicine, and cognitive science, to name a few.

I want to lead off by talking about educational psychology. It's a field with an important calling card often underutilized in both applied and research settings. To be an educational psychologist means that you give priority and attention to the learning environment and the features that promote or inhibit learners from making the most of their time there. I have training in medicine, clinical psychology, and cognitive neuroscience, but I intentionally chose to apply those fields to educational psychology, combining their knowledge bases with neuroscience with the intention of using my synthetic skills to resolve learning issues faced by individuals in both formal and informal learning environments. My clinical skills help me determine the root cause of a problem. But, by simply diagnosing or determining what is disabled, dysfunctional, or underdeveloped, we only have half of the picture. In each case of disability or disease, there are gifts and talents that arise when alternate types of neural processing develop in the face of the organic problem to compensate for and accommodate the diagnosed condition. Whether the talent is an endowment of natural intelligence, a creative skill, or an insatiable motivation to learn, the nervous system has a will to develop even when typical developmental trajectories are off course.

The colloquial version of what I do is study learning from "the outside in" as an educational psychologist and from "the inside out" as a cognitive neuroscientist. As an educational psychologist, I believe that what is off course in our educational processes is "fit." In our public systems we're equality driven—everyone has to achieve the same end, measured by the same test. Teachers and students alike are held accountable in this zero-sum game. People are suffering in the name of education. Suffering to meet and maintain standards and mandates that may not fit our students' mental health, stress, time, and workload needs. It's terrible! But, everyone has had a superlative learning moment. You could tell me a story of a time when the teacher, circumstance, and motivation melded together into a moment of learning alchemy that created more than the sum of its parts. Those shining moments are wonderful and memorable, wherever and whenever they occur. Maybe you had a personal attachment to a teacher who gave extra attention to detail when it came to your interests and questions. Perhaps a teacher assigned an open-ended project that had such rich expectations and clear instructions that you were able to dive right in and enjoy every moment. Or, you had a teacher who always knew how to adapt to their students and taught you and your classmates to do the same. If those kinds of circumstances can only happen by chance, we are doomed. Education is the thing that is supposed to open up opportunity and make everything else better. I hope to help you make small but powerful adjustments that improve your practice one classroom at a time, one student at a time. Systemic education reform may not happen in our lifetime, but people's lives can change every day—for the better. And that includes yours, too. We've forgotten a teacher's mental health in education. Part of the suffering is that a lot of what happens for and on behalf of students happens at a teacher's personal expense.

Fascination with the human brain is evident in our modern culture. Mall bookstores are full of books about the human brain reading, sleeping, gambling, learning, thinking, creating, etc. You can read about the brain from just about any slant. What motivates me to put another book on the shelf?

Part of the goal of this book is to help you set learning conditions, not just teach process. If good education were a recipe, education would be cooking. It would be a consistent process no matter which teacher imparted it. Classrooms would not be vulnerable to differences in resources, social dynamics, or environmental tone.

I think we can agree that education is not just a heuristic or paint-by-number exercise. Good teachers make a difference. So do bad ones.

> *"It only takes a little to set things right."*
> FERGUS WILKS IN GREENFINGERS (2000)

The movie *Greenfingers* is based on a true story of a group of English prisoners who are recruited to create and maintain a garden on the grounds of their minimum-security prison in the Cotswolds. They not only establish a garden, but garner the attention of Georgina Woodhouse, a famous expert, played by Helen Mirren, who shepherds their entry into the world of competitive gardening. The eldest prisoner, who has probably been incarcerated the longest, is a delightful character named Fergus. When we meet Fergus, he has just inherited a new roommate, Colin Briggs, a gentleman who wants nothing to do with his peers. In spite of himself, he ends up befriending Fergus and discovering—by tending to Fergus' hibiscus plant while Fergus lies sick in the infirmary and by accidentally growing a patch of violets that draws the warden's attention—that he has a nascent talent for gardening. At the point in the story when the men have been approached about the garden, Colin is surly and resistant. Fergus looks at him with a twinkle in his eye and says very simply, "Sometimes it only takes a little to set things right."

I tell you this story because it's a good metaphor for what I'm trying to impart in this book. Teachers wear many hats and play many roles. Teaching is like gardening, and you have to tend your classroom and your students as you would a garden. Some of the strategies in the book aren't new; you'll recognize them. They're presented here in light of neuroscience that suggests they are good approaches, and I will explain ways we have misunderstood certain aspects of learning that have kept us from using best practice with more enthusiasm and certainty. Sometimes it only takes a little to set things right. The ideas and science set forth in this book are complex. That is, the knowledge is hard won—combining multiple ways of knowing, concepts, pragmatics, vocabularies, settings, and questions from research in the education, cognitive science, and neuroscience fields. However, the implications for the classroom are often not terribly complex: small changes in practice can have large positive effects. The perspectives and strategies I propose here are intended to reduce stress in the classroom and support the mental health of teachers so that instructional rapport unfolds at its best.

One of the goals of this book is to define and characterize executive functions so they can be taught and coached as an integral part of your instructional style. Differentiation is most commonly executed around content, process, and product. Differentiating to address affect and learning environment don't tend to receive as much emphasis or have as much structure or format. In that respect, they're harder to assess and shape. But interpreting and influencing affect in order to adapt the learning environment is where the real machinery of differentiation lies. One thing that makes this hard to do is the fact that executive functions are in constant development at school ages, and competency varies among children who are typical and/or exceptional in some way (learning disabled or twice exceptional). In general, executive functions fall into two categories: how you manage yourself and how you manage everything else. Because the executive functions are not fully mature in the brain until approximately age 25, teaching and coaching these skills is one of the most important features of education and human development. Yet, how to teach these skills is a hot debate. Good learning psychology suggests that in order to promote learning transfer, these skills should be knit into meaningful and appropriate learning experiences, with lots of practice to apply a skill to varying tasks. Recent emphasis on twenty-first-century skills, such as collaboration, creativity, and innovation capacity, depend on that melded approach, but how to do it best is still in question. Teachers face this dynamic every day. Curriculum and pedagogy can be elegantly mapped, planned, and sequenced, but your students vary in how ready they are each day to learn, how fast they learn, and in what ways they learn best. Teachers have no choice but to confront this mismatch and make continuous adjustments in the classroom. Stored knowledge is the desired output of today's school-based learning environments, at least judging by the standardized assessments used to evaluate student progress. But that's a one-dimensional goal that underutilizes and underestimates many of the features of human memory. Our memory is not designed just to encode and store facts. Our memory holds the formulas for our skills, our habits, our reflexes, our emotional responses, and our perceptions.

When I'm in classrooms, teachers and I are often tackling behaviors and habits that result from an inconsistent executive function: for example, emotion regulation or working memory. Individual differences in the maturation of these functions are a typical part of development, and often an underdeveloped skill is at the root of one of the learning idiosyncrasies that comes with a learning disorder. Leading up to that moment, there will have already been a lengthy evaluation of a student, made up of assessments and observations from the perspectives of the parents and teacher as well as the student—a lot of information about that student gleaned from normed psychological instruments and standardized testing, reported in scaled scores, percentiles, confidence intervals, age and grade equivalencies, and the like. But in that moment in the classroom, watching that student lose track of the directions for the umpteenth time, this is what I often say to the teacher:

> *"This is what you think you see, but here's what's really happening . . . And the next time this behavior occurs, I want you to try A or B and see what happens."*

I can say that to a teacher with a relative degree of certainty because I can better deduce, based on test results, what the root cause of the general behavior is and how to address it. Many times, problems persist in a classroom because the root of the problem is masked. For instance, hyperactivity can have many root causes: a clinically-defined attention disorder (diagnosis that determines hyperactivity is not due to any of the other following reasons), sleep deprivation (organic, family routine, lack of structure), allergy medication (organic), emotional stress (bullying at school or problems at home), or boredom (a mismatch between student ability and/or interest and the current classroom). If a teacher cannot discern the root of hyperactivity, how can they address it?

Why Should You Read This Book?

First, the field of educational neuroscience is in its infancy. We haven't yet achieved the rapport to really marry the fields of education and neuroscience. Cognitive science provides the connective tissue, the opportunity to observe measurable skills and behaviors in a quantifiable way that neuroscience then looks inside at. I hope this book will contribute to the collaboration. I work among the fields of education, medicine, and neuroscience, and while I find it to be an exciting and fulfilling way to work, it's not a comfort zone. Teachers and neuroscientists have a lot to talk about to wrap a collective mind around the right questions and to develop evidence-based practices for education that are informed by neuroscience. As L. W. Green (2008) from the National Institutes of Health so aptly put it,

> *If we want more evidence-based practice, we need more
> practice-based evidence.*

This is where we are in the field. On one side, there is a lot of promising cognitive, developmental, and social neuroscience research; on the other side, there is a lot of good practice and education-based evidence. How to marry the two is still a major dilemma. How do you capture the brain's function in the wild of the real world? How can we take neuroimaging out of the clinical lab? Chapter 3 lends some insight into this.

Second, science maintains a quick clip. I want you to be better prepared to evaluate the science that may support or hinder your teaching practice. When I talk with teachers, I point out that our canons are what I affectionately call "frozen knowledge." The psychological term *crystallized memory* means that a brain can process and recall information that has recognized substance. For example, what is your grandmother's address? Or, what happened in 1776? The question I pose to myself is, how to bring a body of knowledge together in such a way that it remains alive? I have always loved terminology that implies that knowledge is animated: phrases such as *embodied cognition, genetic epistemology,* and *fluid intelligence.* Those terms imply information is lively, viscous, and ever-changing, like we are. There are sayings that we should "be like water," or "bend don't break" to assume any form in adaption to the environment. I'm comfortable with the notion that information lives in fluid forms. That is my experience with it in both in the arts and the sciences.

And so it is with this book, each chapter has a central idea that holds the teaching strategies and the science together in a way that is approachable, graspable, and fun to read. The science is a combination of findings from the cognitive, neuroscience, and education research literatures. In some cases, there are methods may you already know (questioning strategies for example), but I explain the underlying justification that comes from the learning sciences. I will also describe how our nervous system is intrinsically wired in ways that will help you realize that we have misunderstood fundamental aspects of how we are designed to function and treated ourselves counterintuitively. To this end, I will provide stories and details about the relevant experiments and what happened so that you can follow the logic that unravels a previously held assumption or that leads you to realize that you may be overlooking a key moment that would pivot learning in a more profound direction or powerfully seal a social dynamic that results in more comfort and safety. I also want to point out that the references I have provided for experiments, meta-analyses, and reviews have been mindfully curated to provide you with some of the best examples; so if you want to look more closely at good neuroscience, even if the paper is not recent (within the last 5–10 years), you can draw from those. Good papers can be identified by checking for the alignment and consistency of the science: the experimental design is tightly linked to the hypotheses, the study's limitations are clearly provided and addressed wherever possible, and the design addresses the original research question.

Third, it's important to understand that we have one brain. For the sake of clarity, many articles and presentations focus on explaining specific neural pathways, such as those for reading or calculating. But our one brain processes input no matter the source. During learning, our brain's reward systems can be manipulated by substances or influenced by states of motivation and curiosity. Each and both conditions are processed by the brain's dopamine system, which is wired to expect reward and to respond to reward. Early in my training, *Newsweek* magazine published an article on the addicted brain. There was a beautiful schematic image of the human brain with each part of the brain's reward system labeled and clearly explained. I use that image in my talks. And what I point out to my audience is that we could easily erase the tag line of the "addicted brain" and replace it with the "learning brain"—a picture of a motivated, curious, passionate learner. In either state, the same system of the brain gives rise to that recognition and reward.

There are certain paradoxes of brain function that I believe can make a difference in the lives of teachers and students. Teachers have the potential to provide a student with frustration or opportunity every day, and those two states are closer together than you might think. Sometimes they feed each other. We assign value to emotions and feelings that the brain doesn't. Frustration can feel negative and irritating, but in certain contexts this dissonance can also be a signal of impending change. This book teaches you how to use neuroscience knowledge to improve your meta-cognition so that you can use that knowledge to help the learning moment resolve positively even when the mix doesn't seem quite right.

Finally, what if we were to ask the brain what matters most? How does it prefer to be used to promote learning, knowing that it can be used in good ways and bad? This book is about what I think the brain would say. I believe it would tell us it that it wants to be *flexible, ready, connected, and understood*. Understood? By this I don't mean learning the many vocabulary words that identify and label the parts of the human brain; anyone can do that by rote if they choose. Understanding is an entirely different thing. One of the most singular forms of suffering that exists is the feeling of not being seen, of being misunderstood. Neuroscience is teaching us that we misunderstand the way our brains learn in some fundamental ways. I call these *neurological imperatives* for learning that point us to new ways to understand behavior that are just beginning to emerge from the science. These misunderstandings come in the form of behaviors we think we understand, but don't really. What features of learning have we misunderstood? Distraction, mind wandering, teamwork, and the root of individual differences and how to serve them.

This book will introduce you to these facets of learning, what the behaviors look like, what we think we see, and what is really happening, and then link the science to strategies (some familiar and some new) that can be used to better serve these aspects of our learning and influence your approach to differentiation.

Central Tenets: Four Neurological Imperatives

This book is about ideas from neuroscience research that I believe can most effectively be used to increase learning opportunity and quality of life in formal classrooms, informal learning spaces, and in any teachable moment. In keeping with the finding, from psychology and neuroscience, that the mind is most comfortable with three to five points to work with at any given time (Vogel et al., 2005; Cowan, 2000), there are four imperatives that we'll explore:

1. Flexibility
2. Readiness
3. Connection
4. Masking

I chose these because each skill, state, or concept is based on evidence from the cognitive and neurosciences and is ripe for translation and experimentation. I hope that the way I impart each of these ideas doesn't just convey information; I want you to see and feel how each of these ideas and their stories promote the aha moment in which you understand, knowingly and intuitively, how this would immediately apply to you and the students you teach. In each case, these are ideas that I have tested in my own teaching and practice on behalf of families and children. When I ran my laboratory, I was always the first person to participate in each experiment. I wouldn't ask anyone to come and work or volunteer to assist with our science without having, myself, experienced the steps firsthand.

How This Book Is Structured

The structure of each chapter in this book is designed to help immerse you in a teachable moment that goes beyond the words on the page. The best way I could think of to do that was to enlist the help of some friends and colleagues who were willing to share their stories to help make the case for the lesson in each the chapter. The narrative provides living examples, embodied stories of a person or several people that I believe illustrate each imperative. Anchored with the imperative, living examples, and the supporting science, the chapter moves into specific strategies, referred to in the chapters as "Experiments," as ways for you to explore different instructional approaches in your classroom. These strategies will help you understand *differences* in how people learn even when they have the same condition or express similar behavior. These strategies will also help you appreciate that there is some neuroscience knowledge built into the way that we teach school *now*. Along the way, you will find discussions about stress, grouping, creativity, and other hot topics relevant to education today.

Finally, in each chapter there is a section with the heading "Neuromyth Checkpoint." Every scientific finding is ripe for myth because its context matters. In science, the context is held fixed, with the exception of the variable you are manipulating and testing, by an experimental design. In contrast to the experimental process in a laboratory environment, the classroom is a teeming and dynamic environment. One ideal experimental moment may morph quickly and be vulnerable to misinterpretation when the emotional tone, time of day, or topic of interest shifts.

The other thought to keep in mind is that a lot of the data from cognitive neuroscience is correlational. There are only a few concepts in the learning domain that have been teased out at the causative level within laboratory neuroscience: (1) how reading and calculation processes develop in the brain, (2) the basic physical characteristics and stages of the developing brain, (3) information about features of human memory processing, and (4) the development of attention and sensory systems. We are in a moment where experimental design focused on learning in the laboratory is gaining in complexity to more closely resemble conditions in the real world, but the experimental collaboration hasn't yet scaled into partnerships that permit experimental application and hypothesis testing within physical classrooms, schools, and broader education models. Thus, these Neuromyth sections are designed to illustrate where an idea may be ripe for misunderstanding or misinterpretation.

What You Will Gain as a Result

Note that these chapters are written for you as a person as well as for you in your role as a teacher. It seems that, in the interest of improving the social and emotional climate for students, we have largely left the mental health of teachers out of the discussion. What happens for and to students is largely taking place without taking the teacher's quality of life into account. As a teacher, you are a central and reciprocal part of the environment that you set for learning. Among all of the responsibilities that fall to a classroom teacher, I hope that this book will increase your resilience and give you a way to fit yourself back into your pedagogy and learning life, whether you are online or in a classroom, making your learning space and community healthier for everyone.

Finally, one of the biggest motivations for me to write this book is this: Science is an important tool showing us things about ourselves that we could not learn or see otherwise. But, science experiments show us the group *average*. Statistically significant findings are based on the power of the sample size and the grand mean. People are individuals. So, when you are reading a compelling article about an exciting finding from neuroscience, remember that it was gleaned from an average. This book assembles good knowledge from science in service of the individual so that you can apply these strategies and make use of the insights in your own teaching and on your own behalf.

Because of information emerging from the learning sciences, we have an unparalleled opportunity to work with variables in a classroom that can promote optimal learning conditions. I encourage you to view yourself as a "dendritic engineer," because short-term memory and the activities that are happening in your instruction on a daily basis influence what happens to the quality of neural plasticity and the brain's development. And brain development happens no matter what. Time marches on. It is the quality of what happens that determines the quality of how development unfolds. Teachers have students in their charge and in their care for more days of the week, hours of the day, and months of the year than any other person or environment a student will experience outside of life at home. The classroom is a unique opportunity to influence the development of skills that don't just prepare students to pass a test but also give them true performance skills for life. And neuroscience, applied responsibly, can point to ways that we can support learning and development to promote the well-being of our students.

Here is a brief overview of what you will encounter in each chapter. Chapter 1 talks about ways to support the development of cognitive flexibility by leveraging a typically negative quality in the learning environment—distraction—to enhance learning. Similarly, Chapter 2, presents the insight that mind wandering and off-task behavior (other types of typically negative behavior during learning) are, in fact, ingrained processes in our brain that serve learning. In this book, you will learn *how* to value these states and behaviors and *why* they enhance learning. Practicing and developing cognitive flexibility in an environment that promotes and supports readiness allows students to fully open their minds to learning. In Chapter 3, these ideas lead us to the premise that a mind that is secure and fully open can see a bigger picture. A mind in this state is ready for higher-level concept-based learning and can also be open to influences such as inspiration and learning in the service of something greater than oneself. Teams thrive when members have a clear understanding of their collective role, resources, and each other's individual capabilities as they collaborate toward a higher common goal. Not only that, team dynamics can enhance learning, and it is possible to teach and coach the skills of teamwork and collaboration to students who don't come by those attributes and mindsets naturally. Finally, Chapter 4 addresses the subject of masking, that is, how abilities and skills can veil the true roots of intellectual weaknesses, how to recognize the behaviors of executive function, and how to best identify and serve the individual differences in your students. The Conclusion situates the teachings in the book into the context of the pandemic, emphasizing that the neuroscience in each chapter is relevant to all of us as individuals, and that the strategies can be applied during in-person or online learning and in both formal and informal learning contexts.

A Call to Action Research

How do we deepen our understanding of ways neuroscience can support and liberate learning potential in all students? This book is written to increase your metacognitive and reflective capacities as a teacher, to help you develop these qualities in your students, to show you how to adapt strategies you may already have experience with (e.g., questioning strategies, spaced learning) and how to adopt some new ones (e.g., reverse quiz, assessing "teamwork" health) to fit with the knowledge about the neurological imperatives for learning introduced in this book. The neuroscience methods of hyperscanning and group brain dynamics provide an overlap between education practice and neuroscience experimentation, but even those methods are in their infancy in the learning sciences. In the meantime, there is an existing method for you to leverage in your own classroom: action research (Feldman & Minstrell, 2000; Mills, 2000). Playing on the idea of the 3Rs of schooling—reading, writing, and 'rithmetic—Robertson (2000) posed the 3Rs of action research: reciprocity, reflexivity, and reflection-on-reality. Earlier, I referred to a teacher as a dendritic engineer. The evidence throughout this book shows you, in new ways, how important a teacher's role is, both as a person and as an educator. The spirit of the strategies in the book help you place yourself back into the learning context in a way that provides you with moments of insight about and reflection on your own self-care, your practice, and your students, and with increased flexibility in how you respond to your students (reciprocity) and adjust your teaching and curriculum (reflexivity). The concepts "reflection-in-action" (Munby & Russell, 1990), "puzzles of practice" (Munby & Russell, 1990), and robust self-efficacy (Bandura, 1982) come to mind. Bandura's work showed us that high self-efficacy is protective against many forms of stress and can be modeled for others as well as internalized. If you care to engage the principles and strategies in this book in a systematic way as an individual or as a collective group of colleagues, action research is a good place to start because it's a familiar method in education practice that provides a set of steps and expectations to help structure your planning, experimentation, and inquiry.

TEACHING TO EVERY KID'S POTENTIAL

CHAPTER 1

Flexibility

In this chapter, we'll focus on one of the most fundamental executive functions: cognitive flexibility, a hallmark skill of self-management and one of the primary skills impacted by learning and psychiatric conditions such as ADHD and autism spectrum disorders. Keep in mind that executive functions are only fully mature around the age of 25 years old; thus, teachers see the consequences of immature executive function skills every day and observe how they vary among the students in their classrooms. A key feature of the discussion in this chapter has to do with the role that distraction plays in learning. We typically view it as a villain, taking away someone's attention and ability to focus on their learning. Distractibility plagues children with learning and psychiatric disabilities (e.g., ADHD, autism, dyslexia, dysgraphia) and the result can be a marginal school experience at best. Indeed, cognitive flexibility has to do with how well someone can martial their intellectual resources in the face of distraction.

Yet, we are learning from neuroscience that distraction can be used strategically to enhance learning! By teaching you how and when distraction can be a great learning tool, I hope to add to your flexibility to differentiate instruction and turn moments that you currently experience as obstacles into the teachable moments they could be. Also, by using distraction intentionally, you will be shaping how flexible your students can be in both low and high moments of it. Over time they will become more practiced at knowing when it is best to be flexible and when to apply their focus. By doing this, you will help their brains improve how well they contend with things competing for their attention.

What Is Flexibility?

Most of us can probably think of a person who always has the right response in the moment. You may not think of that person as intelligent, but you appreciate that they are always attentive, prepared, responsive, and appropriate. This is someone who has mastered cognitive flexibility. Everything they say and do appears with ease and poise. In plain terms, cognitive flexibility means you use what you have (knowledge, skills, talents) appropriately. In this chapter, we'll explore some of the skills, processes, and products that comprise being "intelligent" and why it is important to revise our conception of intelligence as fixed and to instead understand that our expression of it varies and is influenced by context. By understanding and helping our students understand that intelligence is adaptable, and that the skill of thinking well can be developed and trained, we can unlock powerful new avenues of motivation and sustained learning in the classroom.

Flexible thinking is one of the most important skills a person can cultivate. Why? One of the keys to sustaining learning is our ability to be adaptive and flexible. Cognitive flexibility helps us to move between contexts (e.g., work tasks, home projects, socializing, working solo or in a group), to respond to surprising and unanticipated demands in daily life (i.e., the day that unfolds as opposed to the day that you planned), to work among complex tasks and projects, and to give our attention and emotional resources to the social environment. It's a big skill, one of the eight or nine skills that comprise the brain's executive functions. When psychologists measure it in individuals on certain cognitive tests, it is characterized as the ability to shift from one task to another. The implication is that a student was focused prior to making that shift and was able to re-establish their focus after the shift on the next thing. People practice cognitive flexibility during moments in a group music rehearsal, team sports, or living as a member of a close social community or large family.

Sometimes it matters how quickly you can produce a response or solution to a problem, question, or other demand. For example, when someone volunteers to participate in a neuroimaging experiment, they will be asked to play a computerized game to solve problems and make choices by pressing a button to give their response (yes/no, multiple choice, etc.). These games are delivered by software programs that measure how quickly someone responds in milliseconds. It goes without saying that 1/1000th of a second is a precise measure. But what exactly does a shorter response time mean, and why do we hold thinking fast in such high esteem? Certain professions such as surgery, rescue, trading on the stock floor, professional sports, or driving a race car unarguably require speed and fast reflexes as part of the skills required to be competent and expert. Aside from those contexts, we need to consider that it is equally important to be able to think well—to tackle complex and ambiguous problems with good reasoning skill, creativity, intuition, and thoughtful reflection. Cognitive flexibility is not simply a measure of how fast someone thinks or takes action.

Strategies to Develop Flexibility: An Overview

This chapter describes five approaches that will engineer your classroom to engage your students and develop their cognitive flexibility:

Flexibility Strategy 1: Engage students with joint attention

Magicians and actors use joint attention as part of their craft, to pull rabbits from hats or make you believe in their character. Joint attention is a natural human skill that begins to develop during infancy, when the only communication that is possible happens via gaze and gesture. Babies quickly learn to watch and imitate their caregivers and use their own eyes and hands to orient people to their wants and needs. Joint attention can be used effectively in a classroom to engage students in a new learning experience.

Flexibility Strategy 2: Teach students to "see" time

One of the trials of childhood and the behavioral markers of disability is how children perceive time. Teachers and parents fall victim to the grand power struggle to get children to wake up, get dressed, eat, get to school, finish their work, etc. on time. By teaching them to *see* it, they *learn* time instead of feeling victimized by it.

Flexibility Strategy 3: Use carefully chosen questioning strategies

Questioning strategies can add cohesion to your teaching while you engage students who move at different paces.

Flexibility Strategy 4: Plan a curricular switch

Arranging to teach a lesson out of context in a meaningful way can boost creative flexibility and conceptual learning. When students participate in a topic they have experience with (e.g., performing a science experiment) in a novel context (e.g., an art studio instead of a science lab), they are forced to work on a familiar process in a new situation. This can simultaneously challenge them to adapt their process to the new context and to observe what parts of the process transfer or generalize, which can reinforce and extend aspects of their prior knowledge.

Flexibility Strategy 5: Experiment with spaced learning

Spaced learning teaches you how to use distraction on purpose to promote better memory retention. We are used to thinking of distraction as a negative, but we are learning that it is a natural feature of our human neurology. Thus, it is a fruitless goal in education to try to extinguish it. The utility and purpose of distraction may be the number one misunderstanding we have about ourselves and how our brains are wired. Properly understood, it can be leveraged as an asset. Before we look more deeply at the teaching practices that can help promote cognitive flexibility, let's consider a highly developed example of this executive function skill.

Flexibility in Action: A Portrait

Musician Bill Kirchen has a long-standing career as a Grammy-nominated electric guitarist among folk, classic country, rock, and other forms of Americana roots music. In the early 1970s, his hit song "Hot Rod Lincoln" catapulted his band, Commander Cody and the Lost Airmen, to a Grammy nomination. It is a song that fuses together and then unfolds the sound of nearly every iconic guitarist in recent musical history in quick succession; to name a few in the line-up: Chuck Berry, Deep Purple, The Monkees, Jimi Hendrix, Johnny Cash, Buck Owens, Travis Tritt, Merle Haggard, Earl Scruggs, Bo Diddley, Stevie Ray Vaughan, B. B. King, Elvis Presley, and the Rolling Stones. Bill plays through the song in each of their styles with thrilling effortless aplomb, clearly enjoying his talent for rolling from one of these musical styles to the next with well-calibrated humor and sheer ease. (Interested in seeing him in action? Watch his 2012 performance of the song from a concert in Madrid, Spain, https://www.youtube.com/watch?v=ghz9rCOVHUc)

It clearly took a lot of practice and time to develop the skill to play the guitar and imitate multiple generations and genres of artists with the speed and ease that characterizes "Hot Rod Lincoln." Kirchen's performance horsepower is a striking example of what embodied flexibility looks like when knowledge and skill have been ingrained, well-practiced, and grounded in passion and joy, the combination for gold-standard learning! Yet, in school, Bill describes that he was very often distracted and off-task, much to the chagrin of his teachers.

Bill was one of my teachers at the Augusta Heritage Center in Elkins, West Virginia, during Early Country Music Week in July of 2016. Augusta is a place where musicians in the early root musical traditions come to learn from each other and hone their performances. Bill's class took place in the morning hour just after breakfast. Folks would straggle in from late night music jams with coffee in one hand and a guitar in the other. As a student in Bill's vocal class entitled "Songs From the Wild Side of Life," I quickly learned that he was not only a natural musician, but also a talented teacher. The mix of his musical expertise with a quick wit, larger sense of comic timing and delivery, and empathetic manner makes him a natural teacher, too. Even the sleepiest and most anxious students quickly came around, eager to dig into song lyrics that were new to us but some of the best songs country music could offer from days and greats gone by such as Hank Williams, Lefty Frizzell, Buck Owens, and Kitty Wells. By the week's end, everyone was belting out songs without an inhibition or a care in the world. Bill's facilitation allowed natural leaders in the group to emerge to mentor others along in their skill or their confidence and no one felt left out or behind. The tour de force of the week was a group performance of "Papa Oom Mow Mow," made famous by The Rivingtons and The Beach Boys. The way Bill managed his classroom was a beautiful experience of what it is like when a teacher melts away performance anxiety and barriers to learning using music and humor to establish emotional and intellectual safety among the class participants.

Bill shared a bit about his early education experiences, jokingly explaining that he was the learner that teachers had to duct tape to the chair, and sometimes used the tape to keep his mouth shut! He softens his example, saying that he had a great experience growing up, but that he was not a model student in school. Indeed, there are lots of young, curious, distracted, and more reflective and talented students in classrooms the world over that are surviving school instead of thriving there. Bill describes his own student days as a happy time, but says his behavior challenged his teachers at times because he was often too talkative and social. And yet, that flamboyance and energy are the hallmarks of his charisma with audiences. Underneath his personality is a highly skilled musician who has a command of his craft rivaled by few others. He imparts his skill with humor and fun, but underneath he has a rock-solid grasp of the knowledge and ability that support his carefree manner on stage. So, what does Kirchen's story teach us about acquiring the expertise of cognitive flexibility? Thinking flexibly means that a person can apply and switch among different rules according to what a task requires, even in the face of external distraction.

What We Misunderstand About Distraction and Flexibility

Classrooms are natural places to experience distraction; students get practice at adapting to changing demands during learning. The challenge for a teacher is to establish conditions and create opportunities for learners to respond constructively to tasks and shift appropriately among tasks. Although distraction is sometimes an undesirable and unwelcome state of mind during learning, we are going to see in this chapter how you can use distraction strategically to benefit learning and support the development of cognitive flexibility. A teacher can engineer conditions to promote more flexible and resilient approaches to learning even if the environment is noisy or full of other activities competing for attention. One of the executive functions that bears the weight during content learning (how much information can you work with at once) and determines how well someone deals with distractions from the environment (it is noisy or overwhelming in some way) is working memory. Informally speaking, working memory determines how well we multitask, one form of cognitive flexibility. Working memory is the process that connects what we know to how much of it we can use at one time. For example, seven "slots" are typically available in working memory (Baddeley, 1994; Miller, 1956); this is the wisdom behind 7-digit phone numbers. Visually, people are able to maintain about four objects at one time in working memory, including the position and the color of an object (Luck & Vogel, 1997). As the visual complexity of an object increases, working memory storage capacity decreases, illustrating that this system in the brain is limited to immediate short-term processing (Awh et al., 2007). An important connection to classroom learning and behavior is that *people with lower working memory capacity have a more difficult time filtering out distracting or irrelevant information (*Vogel et al., 2005*)*. A dimension of working memory that has been sorted out by research comes from Fukuda and Vogel (2011) who learned that groups with either high or low working memory skill were *not* different in their susceptibility to distraction, but that the high capacity group *recovered more quickly*. Notably, when given enough time, the low capacity group can reach the *same* level of accuracy as the high capacity group (Heitz & Engle, 2007). Irrelevant information will initially distract or capture the attention of all your students! The difference between groups with high or low working memory skills lies in the *amount of time* they need to disengage from or disregard the distractors. Working memory is one of the skills typically impacted by learning disabilities and second language learning, and it varies among all children (Kalbfleisch, 2013; Kane & Engle, 2002; Miyake & Freedman, 1998). The piece of wisdom that comes from this finding suggests that supporting students processing information at different rates is different from reigning in the attention of students whose curiosity may have moved beyond the lesson.

Calibrate distractions so students can devote their mental energies to learning instead of constantly recovering from interference! I like to refer to this interruption in attention as a *boomerang*—the time it takes to bring a student back from a period of distraction to an attentive and focused state of readiness. A common assumption about students who have slower processing speed and working memory is that they are either not motivated or not trying hard enough. In fact, it's the opposite. Students with immature skills in these areas try harder than their peers with typical abilities for their age (Heitz et al., 2008). What appears to be something they *won't* do is really something they *can't* do. Their boomerangs take longer to reverse course and come back.

An Educator's Experiments

This section presents strategies for you to try in the classroom. Why call them experiments? Because, as I mentioned in the introduction, these are not recipes for learning, but methods for you to try in the spirit of action research, whether you are a beginning teacher or a master. Some strategies will work better than others among different groups of students, some strategies will feel more comfortable to you, and it may take some time for you build new strategies into your routine.

Flexibility Strategy 1:
Orchestrate the learning dynamic using joint attention
Paparella and Freeman (2015) refer to joint attention as an "engagement state": that is, when one child notices another and coordinates their attention with that other person in a shared activity. The quality of joint attention is defined by a number of levels. The most basic form is facilitating someone's attention to an object that is close to them or within their reach. The next level of joint attention is responding to a shared context in some way. Finally, the most robust form of joint attention is initiating or engaging someone's joint attention to focus on a new shared priority. Ways to cultivate these levels of engagement take multiple forms: staying in close proximity to a student to keep them on track by directing their attention with a light touch on the shoulder or their chair or desk, pointing to a specific point on the board, screen, or in the room they should give their attention to, or assigning their attention to another student in the group. These kinds of gentle coordination have been applied to coach attention in children with autism (Paparella & Freeman, 2015; White et al., 2011; Mundy & Newell, 2007) and are often recommended to improve

attentiveness in students struggling with inattention or impulsivity. Joint attention is a way to bring a student back into the moment where you want them to focus on a particular thing. Your relational fluency with your students—how easily you move among them and use your proximity to them to orchestrate individual and group-level attention—is an important part of the routines and climate of your learning space and supports the individual dispositions and abilities of your students.

I recently observed a public middle school language arts classroom filled with 34 students. When I walked in, they were engaged in a noisy boisterous round of a Jeopardy-like quiz game tapping into their knowledge of various writing conventions. Chaos turned to calm when the teacher took a bell chime and mallet out of her back pocket, strolled the center aisle, and rang several times, a sweet light tone that called students to their seats, quieted them, and shifted their attention to instructions for homework.

BOX 1.1: A NOTE FROM THE RESEARCH

One of the delightful findings emerging from neuroscience is that musical training on any instrument, including voice, can enhance the development of executive functions and certain academic skills. For instance, Miendlarzewska and Trost (2014) make the case that successful rhythmic entrainment underlies the far transfer effects that are documented in children, adolescents, and adults alike who have studied a musical instrument. These effects include gains in verbal intelligence, verbal memory, reading ability (Tierney & Kraus, 2013a; Butzlaff, 2000), and in several of the executive functions: cognitive control (Young et al., 2013; Bialystok & DePape, 2009), working memory (Roden et al., 2014), and inhibition and planning (Jaschke et al., 2018). Beat synchronization, the ability to coordinate the tap of your hand or foot to the beat of rhythm you hear, has even been shown to predict reading readiness in preschoolers (Carr et al., 2014). Studies of musical training are showing us that it has a protective effect, that children who are trained in music have an ability to better understand speech in noisy environments and their brains are more resilient to meaningless or irrelevant distraction (Roden et al., 2014; Tierney et al., 2013; Young et al., 2014; Moreno et al., 2011; Bialystok & DePape, 2009).

If you have learners who are naturally distracted, provide a musical catalyst to refocus attention when they are off track or need some fresh motivation. Make shakers—fill plastic eggs with dry beans or rice—a portable inexpensive way to keep musical opportunity nearby. This doesn't have to be intrusive: you set the rules of engagement for how music or rhythm incorporates into your space. For instance, maybe you have a class in the afternoon that is sleepy from eating lunch or maybe it is the last class of the day. Maybe you have been trying to teach part of a lesson or new skill that isn't going very well. Time to use distraction on purpose. You might experiment with a shaker in the classroom and learn that when Johnny is tired or experiencing overload, his concentration is re-energized when he is allowed to "perform" quietly in the background of the class. You impart a leadership role to Johnny by entrusting the learning climate to the person with the shaker. The goal is not to rock out but to use rhythm to synchronize everyone's attention and bring everyone to a state of quiet alertness or soft attention. Everyone else's role is to sit and relax, taking deep breaths in time to the beat of the shaker or a drum. By letting some of the same students begin or using turn taking or allowing students to self-select, you establish a climate of anticipation and relaxation that puts your students into an optimal state of readiness for what you have planned for them. Over time, this routine is something students internalize. You give them a way of regulating their emotions and a way to recover themselves from feelings or distractions that may be in the way of their learning so that they may give their full attention to the present moment. This sense of agency and flexibility is an invaluable tool for your students as well as for you. Using shakers in the classroom won't result in the long lasting training effects neuroscience shows us (see Box 1.1), illustrating that music is an important exercise in developing the flexibility of the brain (Kraus & White-Schwoch, 2020), but including music and rhythm during your teaching is a good way to entrain joint attention and plant the seeds of curiosity and of love for music.

Science Behind the Strategy

RHYTHM. Infants as young as 2 months can discriminate rhythm (Trehub & Hannon, 2006). Seven-month-old infants can detect and follow an underlying beat (Hannon & Johnson, 2005). This kind of informal music making promotes prosocial behavior in children as young as 4 (Kirschner

& Tomasello, 2010) and has been shown to improve language processing in children ages 5 and 6 (Linnavalli et al., 2018). Preliminary studies of synchrony are examining whether it is a natural component of neural processing and what it means when a child is inclined to it or not (Khalil et al., 2013). As a body of work, these studies are showing us that rhythm is one of our fundamental skill endowments in early life. Using rhythm and synchrony in the classroom are logical applications for orienting and influencing joint attention in the classroom.

ENTRAINMENT. One of the ways to model and support positive behavioral conditions is to use entrainment. Entrainment works on the principle that when two energies or frequencies connect that are the same, they resonate and synchronize. When one of the two energies becomes more dominant, the second energy will follow the stronger influence. Does this sound abstract? Music entrains emotional response (Clayton, 2012). So do humming (Osaka et al., 2014), singing, and the sound of the ocean. Sunlight entrains the circadian rhythm in our brains. Jet lag is a visceral example of our circadian rhythms adjusting during travel across time zones. Use entrainment to gain your students' attention and prime their learning readiness with music, humming, rhythm, or your breath. Does this still sound ethereal? There is emerging evidence, based on neuro-imaging techniques called *hyperscanning* and *group brain dynamics*, that illustrates the effects of joint attention and entrainment on learning (Bhat-tacharaya, 2017; Dikker et al., 2017, 2019; Koike et al., 2016; Knoblich et al., 2011). Hyperscanning allows us to see the brain activity of two people simultaneously while they play some kind of game with each other (Babi-loni & Astolfi, 2014). This is an important advance in the effort of neuro-science to capture cognitive activity in a more ecologically valid way or "out in the wild" of the real world. The phrase "the dark matter of social neuroscience" has been used as a way to describe how little we still know about how the brain supports our social encounters (Shilbach et al., 2013).

Flexibility Strategy 2:
Teach your students to see time
One tough aspect of individual differences is how kids sense time. Teach-ers and parents alike hover, cajole, and nudge kids on their way to the next

thing. Wouldn't it be nice if self-regulation could kick in sooner? Helping kids to *see* time will do that and will help develop their planning skills. Keep a set of hourglasses in the classroom. You can buy them in sets that contain 1-, 5-, 10-, 15-, 30-, and 60-minute plastic hourglasses that can survive handling and lots of activity. Begin by introducing the concept with a 1-minute hourglass. Tell your students that instead of lots of rounds of reminders for finishing up work, that you are going to use an hourglass instead, so they can gauge their own progress. Let them know what you expect from them by the time the sand has dropped. Tip the hourglass and have everyone sit quietly to take in how long one minute really is. After that, you set time limits with the other hourglasses as they fit the moment. Each time you use an hourglass, tell the class how long they will be engaged in the task or, if this time is for free choice, how long they will have until it is time to start the next task.

Try opening your class with a 1-minute shaker or a drumbeat. Tell students what you would like from them when the minute is up. For example, do you want them to be seated quietly? Have a certain set of materials ready? Be ready to exit the classroom for something outside, or perhaps the library? Everyone in that environment begins to connect with what a minute really feels like and how long it is. Over time and with practice and repeated exposure from you, they internalize that and develop a better sense of planning, another of the important executive functions, and the time it might take to finish a task. That practice gives them time and multiple attempts to anticipate the shift to the next task, practicing flexibility in a way that is not stressful or alarming. Too often, noises that give a signal—like a class bell or an alarm—can be jarring or startling, particularly if students have become focused on what they are doing. Students with certain disabilities don't react well to those noises, particularly if they are surprising. They will have trouble getting back on track. Teaching your students to *see* time instead engages their sense of anticipation and supports the development of their planning skills.

Science Behind the Strategy
ANTICIPATION. Anticipation enlists the neurochemistry of reward and motivation from the dopamine system instead of causing a flood of adrenaline

or cortisol in response to high stress (Rademacher et al., 2015). Colloquially, it is common to hear, "I just need a minute" when someone is trying to finish what they are doing. Teach your students what that really means and how to use that time effectively. Class time ends without you having to cajole or pester your students to the next task. You literally bring them into an established rhythm that helps to protect them from environmental stress and performance anxiety, to restore alertness, and to support their focus and readiness. Using music, rhythm, and the hourglass technique will help develop the self-regulation that contributes to emotional control and shifting more flexibly among or between tasks—two core executive functions necessary for thinking fast, thinking well, and developing cognitive flexibility.

SELF-REGULATION, INTRINSIC MOTIVATION, AND PLANNING. Planning skills typically require consistent and constant modeling and support in school-aged children because their executive functions are maturing across the years of their education. Learning to plan and sequence information improves, roughly, between the ages of 9 and 17 (Luciana et al., 2009). We live in an age of external stimulation—external reminders, notifications, and alarms chirp from our tablets and smartphones. Thus, it's important to give students the chance to build their regulation capacities from within, and the hourglass strategy provides them with the time and the space to practice within the goals you have helped set for them. Inhibitory control (resisting impulses and the ability to think before acting) and planning are two executive functions that are more closely paired throughout development and begin to braid and influence each other as early as preschool (Carlson et al., 2004). The dropping of sand in an hourglass won't cajole students or interrupt their train of thought. They choose how to spend their allotted time, knowing that at the end they need to have accomplished a certain goal or prepared themselves to move on to something new. When given a goal or task, most people prefer the flexibility of choosing how to accomplish it. Supporting this ethic in students will help build their intrinsic motivation instead of just responding to external contingencies on command. Helping to develop this regulation capacity prepares them for meaningful real-life tasks and models an approach that will help their initiation, or knowing how to get started. A typical refrain from a teacher or parent might be "because I said so," but a steady diet of those kinds of responses doesn't support the development of planning or self-regulation. Teachers and parents alike enjoy the strategy of teaching kids to *see* time because as students learn how to regulate themselves (with time to finish a task or time to prepare for a transition), the power struggles that happen when kids have to be reminded over and over begin to dissolve. Studies of creativity and performance in the workplace have shown that even extrinsic motivators and rewards have their best effect when intrinsic motivation is already high (Amabile, 2018; Gerhart & Fang, 2015).

Flexibility Strategy 3:
Employ questioning strategies to bridge learning differences
CONTEXT MATTERS. To support fluency and recall for both kinds of students (fast thinkers and responders versus reflective thinkers, who take longer to respond), alternate between two questioning strategies: (1) signal students that you are going to question them in one of the next few turns (which gives them time to orient and prepare their minds and responses), or (2) ask a broad conceptual question and then identify a few students you will circle back around to for the answer in a few turns (which gives them time to survey information and generate answers). As your classroom gets used to this strategy, you can designate teams instead of just queuing one person. Using questioning strategies creates greater equity among students as they are given the opportunity to process information according to their natural capacity. Tables 1.1a–1.1c provide a few questioning strategies that have been shown to support achievement and link them to reasons they are learning-friendly from a neuroscience perspective.

Science Behind the Strategy
WORKING MEMORY. Questioning strategies operate on the assumption that there are different ways for an individual to be intelligent. Questioning strategies support working memory in a learner who benefits from reflection time and from help anticipating when to give a formal response. If the bandwidth we have available in working memory were to look like a

pie, meaningless or irrelevant distraction are eating away at the edges of the pie. Kids with attention deficits and autism spectrum disorder and a host of other learning conditions often struggle with working memory, even when they have high capacities for verbal and visual information. They can perceive the lion's share of what is in front of them (visually or aurally), but cannot maintain all of the information in their mind at once in order to manipulate or make use of it during reasoning or problem solving. In the opening discussion on what we misunderstand about distraction and flexibility, I outlined how working memory tends to operate in the brain. This skill can be very different from student to student (Bayliss et al., 2003), and when you have student whose learning tends to bottleneck because they can only work with a small amount of information at once, it can slow the pace of instruction and put that student on the spot because you are waiting for them. Using questioning strategies to orchestrate and synchronize different paces of learning takes the pressure and the attention off of students who need more time to think and reflect and keeps group learning moving forward. In addition, here are four more approaches that support students with slower working memory:

1. Provide information in smaller chunks (no more than four).
2. Provide information visually (color helps collapse visual complexity).
3. Group students according to the speed of their recovery from distraction.
4. Monitor noise levels to avoid competing distractions.

1. Chunking. First, neuroscience studies illustrate that chunking is a strategy that has proven successful for managing a lot of information at one time (Huntley et al., 2017; Prabhakaran et al., 2011). Gobet and colleagues' (2001) definition of a chunk of information is

> *"where each chunk collects a number of pieces of information from the environment into a single unit. The use of chunks explains how greater knowledge can lead to an increased ability*

to extract information from the environment, in spite of constant cognitive limitations." (p. 236)

They point out that one of the best examples of perceptual chunking is how children learn that groups of letters combine to make words. Studies have shown that the brain optimizes this technique by creating one to four chunks of information at a time (Mathy & Feldman, 2012).

2. Going Visual. Second, providing visual information (lists, heuristics, color coding) can boost working memory power or help the brain take another route to problem solving. One neuroimaging study illustrated that when color was included in a visual puzzle, that the brain switched from using working memory systems to the part of the frontal lobes that facilitate our best problem-solving skills (Kalbfleisch et al., 2013). In other words, instead of just weighing the visual load of the puzzle, the brain was able to use additional parts of the frontal lobes to solve the puzzles faster and more easily (Kalbfleisch, 2013).

3. Grouping Students. Third, try differentiating your approach according to your students' ability to bounce back from distraction. In a classroom, we see differences between students who can stay in the moment and keep up with your pace, those who fall behind trying to keep up, and those whose minds wander when things become either too hard or too uninteresting. You could group your students according to these three tendencies (stay in the moment, fall behind due to slower processing, or tendency to mind wander or "tune out") and adjust your pace, supplement your presentation with visual supports, and assign harder questions to the group that needs more challenge to stay engaged. In these ways, you address these individual differences among the whole group instead of approaching differentiation as a load pile-up or too dependent on your direct attention to individual students.

4. Monitoring Noise Levels. Fourth, noise, especially from smart phones and computer notifications, are a competing factor for attention and can be a distraction for all students (Röer et al., 2014). Headphones have become a common way for teachers to help students minimize the effects of background noise. One study that tested the effects of headphones in the workplace found that wearing headphones alone didn't help. Listening to nature sounds provided the greatest benefit to people wearing headphones (Jahncke et al., 2016). Even listening to music has been shown to disrupt quality thinking (Threadgold et al., 2019). New research has determined that speech distractions are not related to individual differences, which suggests that some aspects of distraction are not under voluntary control and that we are all subject to it when noise is a competing factor (Tehan et al., 2018). Although, being able to understand speech in noisy environments is proving to be one of the transfer effects of musical training (Slater et al., 2015).

TABLE 1.1A: Brain-Friendly, Evidence-Based Questioning Strategy: Process

Questioning Process (Bond, 2007)	Rationale	Brain-Friendly Explanation
Write out questions— smart board or PowerPoint—show and hand them out ahead of time, leave them posted	Supports working memory, task monitoring, and planning skills	➤ Create visual support for individual differences: a. Collapse visual complexity to involve the brain's "best" reasoning system b. Boost working memory for students with immature skill c. Promote a sense of anticipation (it fires up the brain's reward system, which stamps the learning moment with curiosity and a desire to see what happens next)
Establish expectations Call on a variety of students Cue students before asking a question Ask questions that are the appropriate level	Promotes equity among students	➤ Create a sense of safety and value with the consistency of expectations. This engages the neurochemistry of connection (serotonin, oxytocin, dopamine) and readiness (the good stress of a little bit of adrenalin)
Ask follow-up questions		➤ Promote an environment that keeps curiosity high for what comes next; keep the brain's reward system ready with anticipation for learning

TABLE 1.1B: Brain-Friendly, Evidence-Based Questioning Strategy: Prompts

Question Prompts (King, 1990)	Strategy	Brain-Friendly Explanation
How would you use . . . to . . . ? *What is a new example of . . . ?* *Explain why . . .* *What do you think would happen if . . . ?* *What is the difference between . . . and . . . ?* *How are . . . and . . . similar?* *What is a possible solution to the problem of . . . ?* *What conclusions can you draw about . . . ?* *How does . . . affect . . . ?* *In your opinion, which is best, . . . or . . . ? Why?*	ROUND 1: Self-guided ROUND 2: Small cooperative group	➤ Initial practice is self-paced and friendly to individual differences ➤ Verbal interaction to support learning ➤ Practice critical thinking vs. rote recall ➤ Creative elaboration and deeper analysis and insight vs. minimal, fact-based explanations

TABLE 1.1C: Brain-Friendly, Evidence-Based Questioning Strategy: Modeling

Problem-Based Learning Prompts (VanTassel-Baska, 2005)	Rationale	Brain-Friendly Explanation
Prompts to introduce a topic ➤ *What do we know?* ➤ *What do we need to know?* ➤ *How can we find out?*	Flexible grouping	➤ Incorporates and includes individual differences
Prompts to deepen understanding ➤ *What is the issue?* ➤ *What and how many perspectives are there on the issue?* ➤ *What are the assumptions of each stakeholder group on the issue?* ➤ *What would be the consequences of each perspective holding sway?*	Supports fluid adaptation and adjustments during differentiation	➤ Promotes the release of neurochemicals in the brain associated with curiosity—dopamine and serotonin

Flexibility Strategy 4:
Develop students' power of observation to promote
skill transfer and develop flexible thinking.

Plan an opportunity with your colleagues to have a *curricular switch* by arranging to teach an art lesson in the science laboratory and a science lesson in the art room. Challenge yourself and a fellow teacher to use only the materials and resources that come with the other's territory. The common thread? The power of observation and how you use that same skill in different contexts.

In science, we use the power of observation to form good working hypotheses. In art, we use the power of observation to create and design. Connecting two subjects that are treated very differently in schools, like art and science, collapses some of the complexity and expectation around what students will gain from a learning experience. For instance, some students are intimidated by science but relish time in the art room. Others like the methodical approach to science and the refinement of routines that characterize a laboratory. While I was designing this approach, I came upon an ideal example that embodies using the power of observation to enhance learning in unexpected ways. One NASA-funded science educator, Adrien Mauduit, leveraged this concept in his own teaching of Combined Science and Mathematics at the Odsherred Efterskole in Denmark (Mauduit, 2016). These courses were compressed, meaning that the amount of content typically taught over a two-year span is taught in only eight months. In order to support students' processing beyond the rote learning required to learn so much content in a shorter amount of time, Adrien enlisted the collaboration of Mette Høst, a visual artist employed at the Niels Bohr Institute, to help scientists visualize new concepts emerging from their work. Using a strategy they called "Visual Science," they required science students to choose drawing, sculpting, or photography to help them reflect and develop a deeper understanding of the scientific concepts embedded in the course content. Picture a physics assignment that asks students to draw or sculpt a physical model of the concept they are working on, or to go out and photograph aspects of the world that portray good examples or powerful analogies illustrating a deeper understanding of a scientific principle. This assignment requires not only flexible thinking, in order to figure out how to artistically portray a science concept, but also a type of perspective-taking to embody that conceptual understanding. Adrien observed that the visual and hands-on components of these artistic approaches resulted in more robust retention and learning compared to those students who chose only the traditional, memorizing forms of engaging with the content. While this example is not the full implementation of the curricular switch, it illustrates the concept of pulling the methods of art into the learning of complex science.

Science Behind the Strategy

NOVELTY. Longtime creativity researcher Dean Keith Simonton and his team showed that diversifying experiences with content during learning can enhance cognitive flexibility (Ritter et al., 2012). By trading spaces and methods for learning (switching the contexts for art and science) you create immediate novelty that helps boost memory. When the experience is fresh and new and you are introducing basic content and tasks, memory is initially enhanced (Schomaker & Meeter, 2015). Dopamine, the neurochemical released when you feel anticipation and reward, is what makes this a powerful way to begin learning (Düzel et al., 2010). Dopamine, combined in just the right amounts with other chemistry, creates an alert (adrenaline) and a desire to take action (acetylcholine) that "embosses" the initial learning, enhancing memory. When the work becomes more complex, the novelty will subside, but by then, deeper learning will already be in process. Novelty will have fulfilled its purpose by jumpstarting motivation and curiosity, and boosting memory associated with the initial stages of learning. Adding to the support for the role of novelty in learning, behavioral activation is a concept from social and personality science that describes what happens when someone participates in goal-directed tasks or assignments and experiences positive feelings when they know there will be a reward for their efforts (Drew, Nijstad, & Baas, 2010). The interesting thing about this and what keeps it from describing whole-hearted extrinsic motivation is that it will only occur when the task is more open-ended and flexible. Behavioral activation does not happen when tasks are more structured and managed. Research on creativity in the workplace also illustrates that introducing a novel way to learn in the form of a seemingly unrelated activity can be both a starting point and an end point for improving affect and motivation (Amabile et al., 2005). That is, that the promise of novel and creative ways to learn can have a positive effect on mood and motivation. That positive effect is then also a by-product of that experience because learning occurred in unexpected ways, engaging in tasks that challenged thinking and required using skills differently or learning new ones. In the case of the curricular switch, what ties the two environments together in the switch is that you are focused on developing the students' powers of observation in these contexts. Because students are practicing the concepts across subjects and environments, the practice not only builds that skill, but helps promote its transfer between those settings and beyond. The second benefit of using novelty as a tool for learning is that it helps instill a mindset based on curiosity and exploration, which has also been shown to enhance longevity later in life (Düzel et al., 2010).

Flexibility Strategy 5:
Use spaced learning to optimize learning and memory.
Spaced learning is a method that capitalizes on the constructive use of distraction. One of the key techniques of spaced learning is the intentional use of distraction at certain points of learning in order to help boost memory and practice shifting from one task to another (Cepeda et al., 2008). Use this strategy when you are in periods of intense direct instruction, such as introducing a new concept or unit or reinforcing core knowledge and skills defined by the curriculum before a test. It has been demonstrated, across many school subjects and with students between third grade and college ages, that irregular spacing between periods of active learning can enhance long-term memory (Smolen et al., 2016; Kelley & Whatson, 2013; Carpenter et al., 2012; Pashler et al., 2007). For instance, in one study from the United Kingdom, a high school biology class implemented a spaced-learning procedure that included a 20-minute period of direct instruction followed by a 10-minute period of distraction during which students were allowed to choose between juggling, playing basketball, or doing an art activity. For classrooms that enlisted this procedure, test scores were significantly higher ($p > 0.00001$) for students who took the national exam

(Kelley & Whatson, 2013). Table 1.2 is designed to help you experiment with spaced learning. It summarizes cognitive studies that demonstrate enhanced learning and memory across different school subjects and at different ages (from fifth grade to college). When Rea and Modigliani (1985) employed spaced learning with third graders who were learning

TABLE 1.2: Examples and outcomes of spaced learning from fifth grade through college

Grade Level	Subject	Timing Gap	Outcomes
Fifth grade	Vocabulary learning (Sobel et al., 2011)	Students were given English words from the Graduate Record Exam (GRE), which were learned in class through direct instruction, slides, oral practice, and paper and pencil tests Immediately following (Group 1) or 1 week after (Group 2) the lesson they practiced the same lesson again Both groups took an exam 5 weeks after the second tutorial	Memory was superior (20.8%) in students who learned with the one-week gap (7.5%).
Eighth grade	U.S. History (Carpenter et al., 2009)	In a spring review at the end of the course, students wrote responses to questions about the content and were given an answer sheet afterward to check their responses Group 1 completed their review 1 week after finishing the course Group 2 completed their review 16 weeks later after returning from summer vacation Groups were tested 9 months after their review	Long-term retention was better for students in the delayed 16-week review, 12.2% versus 8%

High school	Biology (Kelley & Whatson, 2013)	Three 20-minute direct instruction sessions separated by 10-minute distractor periods (juggling, art activity, basketball practice) for a total of 30 minutes	Test scores on the U.K. national curriculum biology exam were significantly higher for spaced learning groups (p > 0.00001)
College	Math learning (Rohrer & Taylor, 2006)	Students were given a tutorial on how to solve a problem and a set of 10 practice problems (0-day spacing gap) or learning was spaced across 2 sessions separated by one week (7-day spacing gap). A test with novel problems was given 1 or 4 weeks later	Spacing did not impact scores on the test 1 week later, but the test scores on the test given 4 weeks after direct instruction were double what students earned after their test one week following direct instruction
Multiple studies reviewed across subjects and school ages to determine optimal principles for spaced learning	Review (Carpenter et al., 2012)	The formula for figuring out the optimal spacing gap for your instruction is: 10–20% of the test delay or the longer the test delay, the longer the spacing gap. For example, for students who complete a final test 7 days after their final study session, the optimal spacing gap is 1 day between the day of direct instruction and the retention test. For students waiting 35 days to take the test, the optimal spacing gap is 11 days.	

to spell and multiply, they observed that spaced learning doubled retention, regardless of their students' ability levels.

Other ways spaced learning could be used in the classroom include quizzing on key concepts several days after teaching these concepts or assigning writing reflections several days after learning. Spaced learning could fit well with patterns of formative assessment that you may already have in place across the curriculum to observe the development of knowledge and skill at different timepoints across learning.

Science Behind the Strategy

TIMING, MEMORY, AND LEARNING. Spaced learning, or the spacing effect, describes an advantage for remembering that happens when students study material on several separate occasions instead of all at once (Sobel, Cepeda & Kapler, 2011). Memory processing in the brain creates what Smolen et al. (2016) call molecular traces of time. When you first learn something—a word, a symbol, or a location, for instance—that moment creates neurochemical and electrical changes in neurons that cement that association into your neural tissue. The technical name for that process is long-term potentiation, or LTP. LTP initiates the process of knowing and then remembering. Like a vibrating string on a guitar, the neurons associated with learning the word "rhinoceros" and remembering it (making the necessary associations to create a robust memory—it's an animal, lives in Africa, has tough gray hide, likes the water) fire and strengthen the physical tissue connections among the neurons in the brain that then retain that memory.

It has been demonstrated, across many school subjects and with students between third grade and college ages, that irregular spacing between periods of active learning can enhance long-term memory (Smolen et al., 2016; Kelley & Whatson, 2013; Carpenter et al., 2012; Pashler et al., 2007). In spite of a fairly large literature on spacing effects that show it can improve memory retention and better titrate the amount of time required for direct instruction, spaced learning has not yet become a mainstream model in the classroom (Kelley & Whatson, 2013; Carpenter et al., 2012, Sobel, Cepeda & Kapler, 2011; Pashler et al., 2007).

However, I offer one example from the literature for your practice because it is succinct but with sufficient detail to describe how you can use spaced learning in the classroom. In this study, the researchers assessed the effects of differently-spaced learning sessions (all in one day versus spaced by 1 week) on the recall of vocabulary definitions after a 5-week retention interval. They made sure that the level of difficulty was the same for both groups.

BOX 1.2: SPACED LEARNING PROCEDURE

This spaced learning procedure (Sobel, Cepeda & Kapler, 2011) consisted of 5 steps taking approximately 15 minutes. Instruction time was 10 minutes for both spaced and massed learning conditions.

Learning Session 1

Step 1: Students received booklets containing four words, their definitions, and use in a sentence. Students read along with the teacher who projected words on a screen, reading definitions and sample sentences aloud once.

Step 2: Students had 3 minutes to complete the first page, writing down definitions for all four words.

Step 3: The next page contained the correct definitions. The teacher repeated definitions and sample sentences. Students had 1 minute to read definitions to themselves.

Step 4: Students had 3 minutes to complete the last page by writing down the definition of each word and a novel sentence. Then, the teacher collected the booklets.

Learning Session 2

Students were re-taught their words repeating the same method from the first session.

Students in the massed condition participated in the second session 1 minute after the first. Students in the spaced condition participated in the second session 1 week after the first.

Testing Retention

Five weeks following session 2, students took a 10-minute vocabulary test consisting of the four words and asked to write the definition for each. Students participated in two test sessions with

> four words, keeping the retention interval equal for massed and spaced conditions.
>
> *Results:* Students in the spaced condition recalled almost three times as many definitions as they did in the massed condition. Re-learning the same material after a 7-day gap resulted in superior performance compared to massed review.

What would the classroom look like if we applied knowledge about individual differences in how fast people process information and the insight that we are all susceptible to distraction? In the classroom, even the working memory capacity of one student inevitably varies as it can be influenced by factors such as health, the time of day, subject matter, and relationships with the teacher and peers. For this reason, faster processing does not necessarily mean smarter. In fact, students with lower working memory capacity or slower processing speeds will arrive at the correct answer if they are provided the time to focus their attention on the relevant information. These are all elements that can influence cognitive flexibility and the quality of learning.

Neuromyth Checkpoint: Assumptions to Question

Until more results from the neuroscience laboratory are tested using in situ classroom research, findings from the learning sciences will remain at the correlational level and perhaps be at risk for overgeneralization and application out of context. The following are a set of assumptions or blind spots to be aware of as you work with the individual differences among your students.

Assumption 1:
A student's intellectual capacity is correlated with the speed of their response and their level of cognitive flexibility.

There are many students who are smart but have slow processing speed or limited working memory capacity. It's common in classrooms to equate smart with fast and to favor the students who have the answers first and typically are not shy about sharing what they know. However, when you have students in your classroom who are quiet and more reflective because of temperament, working memory, or processing speed, it's important for you to have other ways to keep your whole class involved. There is lots of evidence to show how social inequities play out in the classroom and limit achievement of certain students (Oakes, 1990). Students with speed and initiative are rewarded in classrooms that are driven by learning outcomes more than they are by process. But, think about careers that value reflection: research and innovation, creative endeavors, thought leadership. Maintain every student's learning opportunity by varying how you assess their thinking and at what time points you assess what they know. In a balanced classroom, students who think fast and students who think deeply but more slowly have ample opportunities to portray their knowledge—and, with your use of strategic methods will develop collaborative skills. Appreciate how these two forms of performance are assets that complement one another in the service of greater learning.

Assumption 2:
A student cannot learn complex material if basic skills such as spelling or computation are weak.

Some minds require more complexity up front in order to find the content engaging. These students may never spell or calculate well but may very well have the mind that one day solves a great problem. These students may also be more reflective thinkers who require practice and experience with cognitive flexibility. These kinds of students are sometimes referred to as twice exceptional (Kalbfleisch, 2012, 2013), which means they have a clinical or learning impairment but are also highly intelligent and skilled beyond their age and training.

Assumption 3:
Spaced learning is really just a synonym for purposeless distraction.

In the process of executing spaced learning, you introduce intentional periods of off-task behavior for everyone at the same time in order to facilitate memory and learning. You may give students choice in the type of distraction they choose (play, reading, casual socializing), but you structure and schedule it in service of a predetermined schedule.

TAKEAWAYS FOR SMALL BUT POWERFUL CHANGES IN PRACTICE

Here are some takeaways from this chapter to support your in-the-moment strategies for promoting flexibility:

➤ Using distraction in the right way and at the right time can help support memory and learning.

➤ Teach students to *see* time so that they begin to internalize it and get better at self-monitoring.

➤ Students vary in their recovery time from distraction. Naturally flexible learners will recover more quickly; but with time, all students will.

➤ The power of observation can promote skill and knowledge transfer across different domains.

➤ Carefully planned questioning strategies improve cognitive flexibility and help to accommodate, engage, and value fast thinkers and reflective thinkers.

CHAPTER 2

Readiness

One of the features commonly addressed in models of differentiation is learning readiness. Readiness influences how adaptive a student's mind is and the quality of their learning. The premise driving this chapter is the basic human need for a safe and supportive learning environment so that students can settle and open their minds. The challenge for teachers is that a student's sense of safety and well-being is subjective and personal. What challenges and excites one student might be overwhelming to another. At its best, the classroom or a learning space is a place where all students feel comfortable and excited to learn with a greater sense of anticipation than anxiety. In this chapter, I'm going to introduce you to a piece of neuroscience that will change how you view a student's motivation and learning readiness. It is my hope that this insight will allow you to tend a collective feeling of safety and well-being among your students in ways you may not yet have considered.

What Is Readiness?

A person's readiness to learn is influenced by their natural ability, prior experience, and what they already know how to do (Prast et al., 2015; Tomlinson, 2000). When a teacher differentiates content and/or process to address readiness, the optimal result is a student's sense of anticipation for learning because you matched their present learning state. The purpose of this chapter is to teach you to recognize and flexibly respond to behavioral changes that signal readiness during learning as the student's prior knowledge and experience help them adapt and expand their capacities into new learning. To that end, there are learning behaviors in the nervous system that we have misconstrued in the classroom. This chapter features the neuroscience behind a system each of us has called the *resting state*, a system in the brain that constantly integrates information into our minds and bodies and adapts to the demands of our environment and context. It is a system that helps keep the brain flexible, and as it turns out, we have generally misunderstood this fundamental piece of how our brains work. Current education practices that are designed to extinguish off-task behavior (mind wandering, daydreaming, procrastination) work against this part of our nervous system. Our knowledge about the resting state is relatively new. If we can unlearn how we view off-task behavior during learning and then learn to anticipate the kinds of behavior that signal the resting state, then we have room to incorporate strategies into our pedagogy that accommodate the resting state, instead of minimizing it, in the classroom. What would be the result? We would eliminate a current source of stress and anxiety that is provoked by the misinterpretation of behaviors that are actually integral to learning: mind wandering, daydreaming, and procrastination.

Strategies to Develop Readiness: An Overview

Readiness Strategy 1:
Leverage mind wandering for learning—set the pace
Mind wandering can be beneficial in four ways: it can enhance prospection, creativity, meaning making, and mental breaks from tedium or boredom (Smallwood & Schooler, 2014; Mooneyham & Schooler, 2013).

Readiness Strategy 2:
Meditate
Research on meditation training is showing us that it can improve focused attention and lessen mind wandering when it isn't serving learning

(Garrison et al., 2015). Meditation can also have protective effects against stress because it can physically alter the parts of the brain that run the "stress department." Meditation can also support and improve cognitive flexibility (Moore & Malinowski, 2009)!

Readiness Strategy 3:
Walk outside and play

Bratman et al. (2015) compared people who walked in urban environments with people who walked in nature and learned that those who were walking in cities were prone to anxiety because they continued to ruminate on their problems, whereas those walking in nature reported letting go of their cares and being in the moment, enjoying their encounter with nature. Mounting evidence from research points to how the outdoors contributes to creativity and mental and physical health—and that you can access those benefits physically or virtually.

Readiness Strategy 4:
Value creative thought processes—use divergent thinking
strategies to complement more rote forms of learning

We're learning that the resting state is heavily involved in creative thinking. Studies on verbal creativity and creative insight show us how it supports specific kinds of processing. Research on individual differences reports that individual creativity can be predicted from looking at resting state processing and suggests to us what an optimal formula might look like for a creative brain to yield an adaptive and flexible mind.

Readiness in Action: A Portrait

When you encounter stories of great thinkers who had humble beginnings and high-achieving individuals, such as musician Bill Kirchen from the first chapter, you learn that school was not necessarily the place that prepared them for the success they experienced later on. When you look at your students whose minds wander, what's the first thought that comes to mind? Do you think they are the students who appear ready to learn? Not necessarily. Sometimes preparing to be ready is visible, like when someone rehearses and practices, and sometimes it isn't as obvious.

Improvisation, doodling, meditating, dabbling in something new, napping, resting, sitting or playing outside, swimming, driving, or doing other things to mildly procrastinate from what one *should* be doing are some activities that don't look like learning, but this time and activity consolidate things people have already learned into memory, and this time is readying them for new learning and more efficient production. Readiness in action is almost an oxymoron because the processes of readiness I'm about to describe to you occur when people are not taking direct action. To illustrate what I mean, let me tell you the story of neurologist Oliver Sacks. Sacks was a brilliant doctor and a prolific writer, educating his readers about some of the poignant idiosyncrasies of our nervous system in states of wellness and disease. Some of his most popular titles include: *Awakenings* (1973), *The Man Who Mistook His Wife for a Hat* (1985), *An Anthropologist on Mars* (1995), and *Musicophilia: Tales of Music and the Brain* (2007). He lived an enormously productive life. But the reason I bring him to your attention here is because of his favorite pastime. He liked to swim. He says his father introduced him and his siblings to the water from birth and that "swimming is instinctive at this age . . . so we never 'learned' to swim" (Sacks, 1997, p. 44). When he passed away in 2015, several articles of personal accounts were published by people who swam with him, which talked about what they learned from time with him at and in the water. Sacks said sometimes he would write in his head while he was swimming and sometimes not: "I feel I belong in the water—I feel we *all* belong in the water . . . I cease to be a sort of obsessed intellect and a shaky body, and I just become a porpoise" (Wallace-Wells, 2012). The repetition of swimming and the feeling of moving through the water relaxes the body and the mind. This relaxed loosely focused state is when the brain's resting state asserts itself to maintain homeostasis and balance in the brain and in the mind. In this way, rest is not idleness. Sacks and his favorite pastime are perfect examples of the buoyancy that characterizes readiness in action because he was able to describe how swimming relaxed him and set his mind at ease. Sometimes he devised parts of his writing while swimming and sometimes he just "became a porpoise." The balance he describes among these states of play, enjoying and giving into the flow and rhythm of swimming, letting his mind wander and entertaining ideas for his work, illustrates optimal relaxed readiness.

What We Misunderstand About Readiness, Off-Task Behavior, and the Resting State

The resting state is active all the time, responsive and adaptive to goal-oriented processes such as reviewing and executing our to-do and vocabulary lists. It "makes room" for the active skills of the brain by quieting processes that the brain does not need for its immediate task. For instance, when neuroscientists design computer game tasks for people to play in an MRI scanner, such as a calculation task like 4 + 4 = 8, if the task is not challenging and engaging enough for the person, what the scientist sees in the person's brain scan is *not* the brain calculating 4 + 4. Instead, they see an image that reflects the resting state, a combination of brain networks associated with language, self-perception, and sensory processing. The resting state on a functional brain scan consists of areas in the medial temporal lobe, approximately where your temples are, and other brain regions that sit under the crown of your head. Once, or if, the math problems become sufficiently difficult for the person in the MRI scanner, then the part of their brain that does the calculation will appear on the brain scan.

How do you recognize the resting state during learning? It turns out that there is wisdom to the saying "I can do this with my eyes closed," because a person can do a really easy task without involving the goal-oriented "do" system in their brain that usually makes that happen. Think about students who appear distracted or bored in class but still demonstrate their learning when you ask them questions about content or ask them to illustrate or interpret a key point in the lesson and they respond appropriately. You can recognize it in yourself whenever your mind wanders or when you have those moments of thinking about your to-do list or upcoming plans with a loved one while you are supposed to be paying attention to activity going on around you such as a classroom lesson or a meeting. The issue in the classroom is that we tend to censor off-task behavior. We cajole and scold students, trying to call them back to the lesson to pay attention the way we think they should.

The Role of Mind Wandering and Imagination

We are missing an opportunity to deepen student learning if we fail to acknowledge the role of the resting state during instruction and practice.

We are learning from neuroscience that the resting state serves a number of functions that are important to learning and memory, and influence *how well* certain information gets stored into memory (Van Buuren et al., 2019)! The resting state is viewed as one of the ways that new information has the potential to emerge in the mind because of the fluid information trade happening among and between more distant regions of the brain that consolidate and store information in memory. There is an old idea in psychology around "constructive daydreaming" (Singer, 1975), the notion that mind wandering could be restorative and fruitful for thinking. Some surmise that the resting state might be where imagination comes from because it responds and adapts to learning processes when someone is doing something that requires effort (Agnati et al., 2013). It is even thought that the resting state influences cognitive flexibility because the types of planning, auditioning, and imagining that occur during mind wandering create a bridge between the present and the future (Roberts et al., 2017; Szpunar et al., 2014; Immordino-Yang et al., 2012; Buckner & Carroll, 2007; Suddendorf & Corballis, 2007). And a big part of readiness involves toggling between the present (what you know and know how to do) and what's coming next (applying your knowledge and skills appropriately to new contexts).

The resting state system has a lot to do with how ready a person is to learn, to receive information, or to try something new. Unlike effortful brain systems and skills that involve the *doing* of things like reading, writing, calculating, problem solving, etc., the resting state, to the naked eye, appears to be more passive. Think of it as the brain's autonomic system, the functional system that helps the brain maintain its homeostasis or balance. Compare it to the respiration in your lungs or the beat of your heart. You don't have to tell your lungs to breathe or your heart to beat. Like these functions, the resting state is not something that you tell your brain to do, it's something it does naturally on its own.

The Resting State Can Enhance Executive Functioning

Recent neuroscience research shows that the resting state can enhance our executive functions during problem-solving and intellectual work (Van den Heuvel et al., 2009). This is important because executive functions are *how* the brain uses its skills and talents. A central theme of this book is to emphasize the importance of executive functions in learning and to present strategies that wittingly help you develop those capacities in your students. It is educationally important to acknowledge and support resting state functions of the brain because mounting evidence from neuroscience shows that the resting state exerts influence on executive functions, memory retrieval, imaginative processes, and cognitive control—how well you can resist interference (Feng et al., 2019). The behavioral feature of the resting state that teachers are most familiar with is mind wandering, which can take place at times that appear to obstruct or be counterproductive to learning. When students aren't challenged, their minds wander. Mind wandering improves mood when someone is faced with a boring task (Smallwood & Schooler, 2010). But the resting state does much more than bolster mood in a boring moment. Table 2.1 gives a summary of how the resting state supports learning and the brain's ability to be adaptive. These are all processes that the brain relies on to ready itself for new learning. When the right balance is struck, students can give their full attention, curiosity, and motivation to the learning moment.

TABLE 2.1: The Resting State and Learning

Ways the Resting State Supports Learning and Helps Maintain an Adaptive Brain
Supports cognitive flexibility—the planning and daydreaming that occur during the resting state provide a way for the mind to switch between the present and the future
Serves as a gateway for new thinking to emerge during problem solving and imagination
Supports thinking that leads to creative insight, idea generation and evaluation, and verbal creativity

Your students do not give you 100% of their attention all of the time, even when you require it most. You know this, but you may not have realized why. In fact, several studies report that most people spend between 25% and 50% of their time thinking about past or future events (Kane et al., 2017; Killingsworth & Gilbert, 2010; Smallwood & Schooler, 2014). That being the case, we need to account for it in our approaches to learning instead of trying to extinguish its influence during student learning. Today's classrooms are organized to teach with an emphasis on high stakes testing performance. The underlying assumption that kids have to learn incrementally and at a similar pace in order to guarantee their achievement sounds logical. But it doesn't stand up to the realities of individual differences (Tomlinson & Kalbfleisch, 1998).

The fMRI picture of the resting state is sometimes described as a picture of what the brain looks like when it is talking to itself. The brain is wired for stories. If none are available, it makes up its own (Kalbfleisch, October, 2009). In light of this, efforts to discipline passive forms of off-task behavior in classrooms have persistently worked against this fundamental aspect of our human neurology. Our knowledge about the resting state is relatively new. In teaching, if we can anticipate the behaviors that signal its function and incorporate strategies into our pedagogy that accommodate it in the classroom, we eliminate the stress that results from the misinterpretation of learning behavior during moments that are actually integral to student learning and are supporting the brain's ability to adapt.

By misinterpreting resting state behavior during learning, we have unwittingly created stress and anxiety during key moments. Use these strategies to insert supportive moments that used to be filled with concern and discipline intended to prevent or interrupt off-task behavior. If classroom practice concertedly involved the support of resting state behavior for better support of executive functioning and adaptive skills, we could optimize cognitive development and support mental health in students of all school ages by teaching them how to recognize and befriend the resting state. And this applies to you, too!

An Educator's Experiments

Readiness Strategy 1:
Leverage mind wandering for learning

Mind wandering can be beneficial in four ways: It can enhance prospection, creativity, problem solving, meaning making, and mental breaks (Smallwood & Schooler, 2014). Table 2.2 presents and defines each benefit and provides examples of how to apply it.

Imagine presenting these four ways that mind wandering can be healthy to your students and having a groundbreaking discussion on mind wandering to let them know how much of a human quality it is and

TABLE 2.2: Mind Wandering Can Be Useful in Four Ways

Processes	Definition/Principle	Example
Prospection	Thinking about the future and comparing and contrasting options for problem solving or visualizing new possibilities	Use thinking models such as compare/contrast; pro/con; cost/benefit; venn diagram or other forms of mapping thoughts to help students find substance in their brainstorming
	Precursor to planning	Prospection is the opportunity for you to help a student see themselves in their learning, to connect to content in a personal way that will help them develop knowledge and skill. If they can see themselves in the picture, they can grasp information in a different way than just using rote memory
Creativity	Increases when mind wandering involves tinkering	Tinker with your mind—divergent thinking strategies such as SCAMPER; synectics; direct analogies, personal analogies, compressed conflicts (Starko, 2017) Tinker with your hands—manipulatives, models, technology
Meaning-Making/Problem Solving	Studies report positive correlations among tendencies for mind wandering and measures that assess an individual's capacity for incubating novel solutions or insights (Baird et al., 2012; Beaty et al., 2014)	Utilize methods from Chapter 1 to support the rhythms of this kind of thought process
Mental Breaks	A pause from direct instruction or goal-oriented learning	Create ways for mental breaks to happen naturally and be used productively, give them a place in the learning process with spaced learning or techniques suggested for planning for spontaneity (stations, library, walk, meditation, yoga)

how you are going to incorporate it into their learning. You become the coach, asking questions when students exhibit mind wandering—"Susie, are you thinking about the future, a solution to a problem (prospection or creativity), taking a mental break so you can make sense of the task, or refreshing your mind to get ready for the next thing?" No blame, no added stress, and no power struggles ensue as you help students make connections between their resting state behavior and their classroom learning, giving them words to understand what processes they are experiencing and how these benefit their thinking.

Science Behind the Strategy

MIND WANDERING AND ACADEMIC PERFORMANCE. Two examples from research support optimizing mind wandering strategies. First, McVay and Kane (2012), determined that mind wandering is a factor in the relationship between working memory capacity and reading comprehension, suggesting that an ability to control attention to intruding thoughts—distractions—is a mediator of successful reading comprehension. The difference between welcome and intruding distractions is how they are used and whether or not you can get a hold of them. Distraction is typically unwelcome. Chapter 1 introduced ways that we can actually use it to enhance learning. This chapter is about befriending mind wandering to reduce stress and realize that it can be harnessed to support thinking. Second, Lindquist and McLean (2011) found that memory retention and test performance in a group of college students during a psychology lecture course was influenced by where they were seated. Students seated in the front third of the lecture hall experienced fewer intruding distracting thoughts than students seated further back in the room. They observed that the number of intruding distracting thoughts was negatively correlated with student age, interest in the course, and the amount of detail in class notes. Furthermore, higher numbers of intruding distracting thoughts corresponded with poorer test performance and lower exam scores. This may spur you to think about ways to eliminate the front and back of your classroom, perhaps by grouping desks. Become comfortable with providing instruction from multiple locations in the classroom so that students aren't vulnerable to the back-of-the-room effect.

On a deeper cognitive level, understand that the mind is, during resting state moments, readying itself to re-engage some aspect of executive function, such as attention or planning.

MIND WANDERING AND EXECUTIVE CONTROL. Neuroscience illustrates a relationship between mind wandering and executive control (McVay & Kane, 2009, 2012; Kane & McVay, 2012; Mrazek et al., 2012; Smallwood & Schooler, 2014). Resting state activity during mind wandering includes reflecting on memories and planning for the future. Research is demonstrating that these processes occur symbiotically and even simultaneously with metacognitive processes, which exert more mental control but also involve self-referential thinking (Fox & Christoff, 2018). Research provides examples of trial-and-error and musical improvisation, which require spontaneity and control. This helps make the case for why resting state processes should be as important as teaching students how to think about their thinking, which involves activities such as evaluating ideas, discerning choices, and being self-aware in the learning moment. As author J. R. R. Tolkien once said (1954), "Not all who wander are lost." How teachers respond to resting state behavior can influence the learning dynamic. Recognizing resting state behaviors provide you with the opportunity to support the brain's ability to adapt and switch between systems that support learning, memory, and executive functions.

Readiness Strategy 2:
Meditate

Research on meditation training is also producing evidence that mindfulness meditation can improve focused attention and lessen mind wandering that is not related to learning (Garrison et al., 2015). Meditation readies the mind. Distraction still occurs, but your mind settles into a choice to regard or disregard it. Distraction, as we learned in Chapter 1, can be beneficial when we use it as a tool in opportune moments. The choice is to resist distraction or use it to benefit learning. The resting state is constantly working under the surface to integrate your experience and cognitive processing. It also features prominently in how we learn and become successful at mindfulness meditation (Moore & Malinowski, 2009). Mindfulness meditation is a type of training that helps you improve and enhance attention, emotion regulation, and other self-regulation capacities (Tang et al., 2015). It has been posed as the antidote to counterproductive mind wandering (Mrazek, Smallwood & Schooler, 2012). It is one of the ways that you can develop a relationship with your resting state because it teaches you how to become aware of the changing states in your mind and integrate them to improve your thought capacity.

Schools are just beginning to incorporate meditation practices into the curriculum, and the results are encouraging. For instance, Robert W. Coleman Elementary school in Baltimore, Maryland, was featured in the national media in November 2016, featuring their self-regulation program in detention, and in the regular classroom, as a means of coaching students to better handle their emotions, a key feature that influences the development of other executive functions and problem-solving skills (Bloom, 2016). In 2019, Patterson High School in Baltimore, Maryland, was also featured in the media for their partnership with a local nonprofit, Holistic Life Foundation, which introduced a Mindful Moment room into the school, a place described as an oasis of calm where students could be referred to, or self-refer, to calm down and regroup (Gonzales, 2019). Their process goes like this: they encounter a Mindfulness Instructor in the Mindful Moment room and engage in a 5-minute conversation to determine their needs and then a 15-minute mindfulness practice that may take the form of breathing exercises or yoga. Once students leave the Mindful Moment room, they are on their way to learning how to reset and de-escalate their emotions before they are overwhelmed by them. At Patterson High School, 30 different ethnicities and over 20 different languages are represented. In the first year of implementing the program, suspensions and verbal and physical confrontations decreased by over half, while attendance, grade promotion, and GPA all increased. A meditation practice in school is a great way to help students develop and gain control over their attention processes. This basic control—to assert your attention where you want it and when you need it—is key to optimizing learning.

Science Behind the Strategy

MINDFULNESS MEDITATION. It makes sense that what emerges from successful mindfulness meditation is a capacity to exert control over your mind in the service of many kinds of learning activities, not just for learning metacognitive skills. Mindfulness meditation has been shown to increase cognitive flexibility and is a neutral way to reach kids and teach them self-regulation skills (Moore & Malinowski, 2009). How do its effects transfer to other tasks and situations? One study presented the idea that both mind wandering and metacognition occur during mindfulness meditation (Fox & Christoff, 2018). While spontaneous emotional reactions and thinking arise as the mind wanders, so do metacognitive tendencies to monitor and catch one's own attention in order to practice a neutral stance. In that time and space, the mind, like a muscle, is developing fluid switching-capacity between these two states. As that muscle becomes stronger, the element of flexibility begins to be maintained outside the practice of mindfulness meditation. The physical basis of these changes appears in the efficiency of the brain's white matter, which consists of the long, threadlike pathways that connect major regions of the brain (Tang et al., 2012) and support the development of executive functions as they mature and integrate into the frontal lobes throughout adolescence and young adult life (Blakemore & Choudhury, 2006). A study that examined correlations among the neural systems involved in meditation, psychotherapy, pharmacotherapy, and placebo discovered that meditation and psychotherapy work through similar actions in the brain (Chiesa, Brambilla & Serretti, 2010). The gold nugget in this finding is that meditation can be done with groups of people, or students, to provide relief and to support mental health outside of classically therapeutic modalities and settings. One of the reasons these approaches appear to work is that they engage the top-down mechanisms of attention in the frontal lobes of the brain that can buffer or diminish the hair-trigger sensitivity of the amygdala, the part of the brain sensitive to stress (Hölzel et al., 2010). Imagine the effect of top-down attention as an oven mitt on your hand trying to smother a hot coal. That top-down effect of grabbing and surrounding the hot coal is what this kind of attention does to surround and muffle a stress response.

Another study determined that mindfulness meditation begins to change the brain physically and chemically within 3 days (Creswell et al., 2016). Even better, 4 months after training, the effects of training were still present in the brain and in people's behavior—they had formed a new habit. The resting state changes in these people's brains accounted for 30% of the new changes in the brain and was associated with a chemical marker for inflammation, which was reduced. Another study showed that long-term practice led to changes in the resting state that persisted even when people were not directly meditating (Jang et al., 2011). Draw a line in your mind that connects mindfulness meditation with changes in the resting state that correlate with improved self-regulation, attention, cognitive flexibility, and reduced levels of inflammation in the body. This is a practice that yields lasting dividends for both learning and health! Not only that, it optimizes the ability of your mind to learn to wield mind wandering as a tool, learning the difference between avoidance and seeking relief from boredom or tedium and engaging the imagination to plan, create, or problem-solve.

Readiness Strategy 3:
Make routine time to play and experience nature (real or virtual)

Keeping your students in what I call a state of play is one of the single best things you can do for their learning. Pellis et al. (2010) advanced a compelling idea they coined, "the training for the unexpected hypothesis," meaning that experiencing the unexpected improves self-regulation. For instance, animals that play are less fearful of and less affected by unexpected events. They don't startle as easily. Their emotional responses are more even in the face of novel events, surprise, or challenge. We need to keep recess!

As we adapt our pedagogy and instruction to the pandemic, one of the ways we can stay healthy is to get outside into the open air and move! If you cannot get outside, it appears that the effects of *viewing* nature can be strong enough—that devising ways for students to access nature, even if it has to be via computer (images, webcam, documentary footage)—can enhance the brain's recovery from recent trauma or upset (Brown, Barton & Gladwell, 2013). For instance, the show *Sunrise Earth* produced by the Discovery Channel (and available on YouTube) is made up of 45-minute episodes that are unnarrated and show the sunrise in several remote locations around the globe (for example, a Mediterranean fishing village or a river scene in the Alaskan wilderness). Only the natural sounds at sunrise are audible. In my practice, I have had success helping kids who have a hard time getting organized and motivated in the morning form a new routine by scheduling their morning preparations to be completed within an episode of *Sunrise Earth*. The instructions to the student are simple: When you get up to start your day, begin playing an episode. By the time the episode is over, be up, dressed, out of your room and ready to go.

Physical exercise is a known way to help the body get rid of stress, so the influence of the type of environment may be a new and important distinction to maintain mental health. For example, students and teachers at the Ideaventions Academy for Math and Science in Reston, Virginia begin the day with a walk in the woods that surround their school building. Students can opt to go fast or slow, sprint or stroll. The physical exercise wakes everyone up, gets rid of any stress left over from the morning's preparations, allows time for mind wandering and play, and puts everyone on the same page to start the learning day. Walks also provide the time to check-in with each other, creating supportive social connection. A chance for you and students to connect on a personal level outside of the classroom brings you back in the door ready to get down to work. As a class, devise alternate activities for days when a walk isn't possible.

Science Behind the Strategy

WALKING IN NATURE VERSUS URBAN SETTINGS. Bratman et al. (2015) compared people who walked in urban environments with people who walked in nature and learned that those who walked in cities were prone to anxiety because they continued to ruminate on their problems, whereas those who walked in nature reported letting go of their cares, staying in the moment to enjoy their encounter with nature. Time in or exposed to nature improves mood, well-being, and reduces negative perspective. This finding was vetted in a meta-analysis that looked at the positive and negative effects of being in natural environments across 32 studies involving a total of over 2,300 participants (McMahan & Estes, 2015). Another study reported the positive effects of extended time in nature over 4 days on creative problem solving and reasoning (Atchley et al., 2012). People walking about cities didn't report the same benefit. In this study, people walking about in cities, which is good exercise and, on the surface, good for stress release, continued to wind up their anxieties instead of diminishing them. We know that no matter how old you are exercise is important to release stress and that being in motion helps encode and consolidate certain types of memory (Lundbye-Jensen et al., 2017; Pesce et al., 2009). But stressful emotions can keep new information out of the brain. There is a recent epidemiological study based on over 900,000 people in Denmark that analyzed the association between living in/near greenspace and the likelihood of developing mental illness. In their data, children who had the least exposure to living in or near greenspace were up to 55% more likely to develop mental illness than children who did. This result remained even after the data was adjusted to explore whether urbanization, socio-economic factors, parental history of mental illness, or parental age were underlying influences (Engemann et al., 2019).

VIEWING NATURE SCENES ON A COMPUTER. One provocative study was able to show that even just viewing nature scenes on a computer can help the nervous system recover (reduce resting heart rate and blood pressure) from recent trauma or upset (Brown, Barton & Gladwell, 2013). It is neat how this team designed their experiment to tease apart which effects of being outdoors are related to exercise, which has known benefits to mindset and health, versus which effects are related to the visual sensory impact of experiencing it. This is a promising distinction for stress relief in live classrooms and remote learning. There are many open source videos of various lengths that can be used to help a student calm down and settle back in to learning.

Eastern and Western medicine traditions include visual imagery among their healing modalities (Sheikh, 2003). Virtual visual feedback has even become a way to relieve amputees of pain they experience from feeling their phantom limbs (Mercier & Sirigu, 2009). One study demonstrates that our visual sense is so strong that when people are experiencing blindness, their visual cortices will become active when only given verbal input (Lambert et al., 2004). The *Science Behind the Strategy* from Strategy 4 in Chapter 3 goes into more detail about the science behind the idea that one of our senses can be used to override sensory or emotional pain coming from another source in our minds or bodies.

MAKING ART. Indoors or out, art is another way we can encourage play. One study examining the effects of art making on stress involved 39 adults, ages 18–59, in an art class and tested their salivary cortisol before and after the 45-minute session (Kaimal et al., 2016). Salivary cortisol is a simple way to measure stress, by taking a swab of saliva from inside one's cheek (Vining et al., 1983). In studio, these participants had the choice of making a collage, sculpting with clay, or drawing with markers. There was a significant reduction in cortisol in 75% of their participants. This happened regardless of demographics, prior art experience, time of day, or choice of art media. People commonly expressed how relaxed they felt, how they were able to lose themselves in the activity, that their imagination was fully engaged, and that their sense of time changed while they were playing. Play is good practice and preparation for life because the risk is low, and you have a chance to learn from your experience and try again. High cortisol levels in preschool children are associated with poorer executive functioning (Wagner et al., 2016). When, if not in school-aged years, is it important to enjoy the safe, comfortable, expansive feeling of play? It's always important. When else do you get to imagine, practice, experiment, and refine what you know, what you do, and what you love?

Readiness Strategy 4:
Value creative thought processes—use divergent thinking
strategies to complement more rote forms of learning.
We're learning that the resting state is heavily involved in creative thinking and idea generation. Studies on verbal creativity and moments of creative insight show us how the resting state supports specific kinds of processing. Research on individual differences report that individual creativity can be predicted from looking at resting state processing. Can you train someone to be creative? That is a longstanding question. But I believe the importance of using divergent and creative thinking strategies may not be for their own sake, or for producing Big C creativity. I think the purpose of these strategies has to do with the larger goal of developing adaptive skills, because part of the ability to adapt is to be open to novelty and to be able to respond constructively to it (Kalbfleisch, 2009). In Chapter 1, I talked about how the mark of real intelligence is someone's capacity to respond appropriately to any moment. That requires flexibility. And what creative thinking strategies appear to do for the brain is create a framework that holds space for the resting state (reflecting on the past and future) and for more direct memory processes to comingle (applying what you know to a novel situation or task) to produce a novel or, at

least, desired outcome. Table 2.2 suggests a number of divergent thinking strategies (SCAMPER, synectics, analogies, and compressed conflicts) for breaking open thinking and idea generation. These strategies don't take hours out of instruction time. Better yet, steady and routine use of these processes trains students to think in open-ended ways, like those that occur in response to rudimentary prompts like compare and contrast, and supports working memory associated with connecting known and novel elements in one's mind.

Science Behind the Strategy

RESTING STATE AND CREATIVE THINKING. The same study that posed a relationship between mind wandering and metacognition in mindfulness meditation also provided an example of this relationship during creative thinking (Fox & Christoff, 2018). Elements of mind wandering that occur during creative thinking include the spontaneous generation of ideas, imagery, verse, music, solutions, and insight, while elements of metacognition that occur during creative thinking involve monitoring the effectiveness of the creative process and evaluating components of the process such as the novelty, quality, utility, and perceived value of the solution. Other studies provide evidence that the resting state interacts with executive control systems not only during creative thinking, but also in specific instances, such as poetry composition, musical improvisation, the making of visual art, and during other exercises of verbal creativity (Feng et al., 2019; Beaty et al., 2016). Resting state activity appears during the generation of ideas and helps your brain flexibly match them with information you already have in long-term memory. These studies show us that the utility of creative and divergent thinking extends far beyond the goals of insight and the aha moment. They are far more pragmatic than we have imagined and, at least to me, appear to the be the other half that completes whole learning—to develop not only knowledge and skills but also the capacities to draw on those in expected and unexpected ways.

Neuromyth Checkpoint: Assumptions to Question

Assumption 1:
The resting state is just a synonym for off-task or undisciplined behavior.
On the contrary, it is not a passive state where nothing happens, but a state that occurs internally, in reference to, but apart from effortful cognition and broad attention. Resting state periods can be accommodated in the classroom. Additionally, strategies mentioned in this chapter help you reframe how you view and use mind wandering to benefit student learning. One of the most important aspects of this insight is that prospection during mind wandering can prepare or ready a student for activities that give them a chance to practice and develop executive functioning skills such as planning and flexible thinking related to creativity and imagination.

Assumption 2:
Mind wandering and distraction are always positive.
When these two states of mind become chronic and consistent, they lose their potency. Mrazek et al. (2012) demonstrated that an individual's frequency of mind wandering was predictive of negative performance on the SAT and difficulties with working memory. This illustrates the complexities of mind wandering and distraction. Both can be counterproductive when they are persistent. With the knowledge about the resting state in hand, you now know that those mind states can be supportive of learning when they are shaped properly and introduced or noticed at the right times.

A startling report of 11 studies on sitting and doing "nothing" revealed that people would much rather do a mundane task than sit alone with their thoughts for 6 to 15 minutes. When they were challenged to sit with their thoughts, they voluntarily administered electric shocks to themselves to disrupt the monotony (Wilson et al., 2014)! This really speaks to the value of cultivating an appreciation for the resting state and reassuring those who don't like to be idle that what happens when they are idle can be beneficial. The fact that some people would rather shock themselves than sit quietly for a period of time begs the point of this chapter: that we have been missing the boat about why, how, and when to include creative and divergent thinking methods into routine practice. And this emphasizes the contribution that neuroscience is making to education; having identified the resting state, this invisible aspect of our brain function that influences the quality of learning.

Assumption 3:
Meditation always results in a positive state of mind.

Be sure to check on students: if they are physically still but their mind tends to ruminate instead of relax, this can cancel out the positive effects of meditation and negatively affect their mental health and classroom performance and behavior.

TAKEAWAYS FOR SMALL BUT POWERFUL CHANGES IN PRACTICE

Here are some takeaways from this chapter to support your in-the-moment strategies for promoting readiness:

➤ Mind wandering, procrastination, and certain kinds of off-task behavior can be beneficial to the processes of learning and creativity.

➤ Recognizing that these processes can be aspects of the brain's resting state allows you to reframe moments that appear unproductive and capitalize on these kinds of down time for better quality learning and classroom environment.

➤ Play prepares people to deal constructively and appropriately with the novel and unexpected.

➤ The ultimate goal of learning is to attain and develop not only knowledge and skill, but also the flexibility to be ready to adapt and apply knowledge and skill during expected and unexpected moments.

CHAPTER 3

Connection

One of the vulnerabilities that children and teachers alike suffer is the lack of a good match in a classroom. Everyone has a memory of a year in their education when they didn't like or didn't work the same way as their teacher, or they believed that their teacher didn't understand how they worked. This sense of incompatibility colors everything. An ongoing conflict with a friend or classmate can have the same impact. The topic of this chapter is connection and the importance of teams during learning. Teams thrive when they have a clear understanding of their role, their resources, and each other's capabilities as they collaborate toward a common goal. Classrooms are teams. You are a team leader. How do you create an emotional climate in the classroom that promotes and maintains a strong sense of connection among you and your students? Is it possible to flatten the hierarchy between you and your students and still be productive? As a teacher, you are part meteorologist (are there still waters, stormy moods, or sunny dispositions in your classroom?), part engineer (features and facets of your curriculum and pedagogy), and part orchestrator of your learning environment (using differentiation). Your leadership skills are important. I'm going to introduce strategies and ideas in this chapter to help you to inoculate your classroom against the potential stress of a mismatch or lack of connection between teacher and student and/or among students.

Here, we delve into the neuroscience research related to social learning and the value of teamwork and empathy.

What is Connection?

The Cambridge Dictionary defines connection as the relationship of a person, thing, or behavior to someone or something else and as the act of joining or being joined to something else. Neuroscientists Naomi Eisenberger and Steve Cole define social connection as the experience of feeling close and connected to others—feeling loved, cared for, and valued (Eisenberger & Cole, 2012). By way of introduction, allow me to describe an example of what happens when people connect in the service of something greater than themselves. By this, I mean living and learning with a goal in mind that serves more than yourself and the moment. Looking back in our continent's history, the villages in Chaco Canyon National Park in Nageezi, New Mexico, stand out as an amazing example of sustained social connection, collaboration, and engineering that took place over decades, creating a thriving center of trade, commerce, worship, science, art, and agrarian life. Located outside of Nageezi, New Mexico, in the Four Corners region of the southwestern United States, Chaco Canyon is a National Historic Park and UNESCO World Heritage site. As one example of the value of connection in learning, it took 11 generations of intergenerational apprenticeship to establish the villages in Chaco Canyon. I often wonder what it would have been like to be the first generation there. Who could have possibly imagined what the 11th would finally finish? The village sites are beautifully blueprinted and complex (see Figure 3.1).

The physical features of the ruins that exist today are only the basic foundations of the old villages. This impressive network of villages has survived hundreds of years past the lifetimes of the people that made them. The ruins leave a record of what was happening with the seasons and the stars as their rhythms guided planting, harvesting, worship, culture, and the schedules of community life. Artifacts all over the surface of our planet stand testimony to how wildly important human ingenuity and problem solving have always been. But those 11 generations of architects, artists, healers, teachers, designers, engineers, farmers, astronomers, masons, builders, and others who participated in the construction

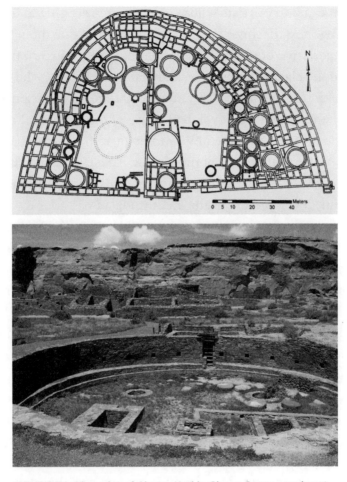

FIGURE 3.1: Blueprint of Chetro Ketl in Chaco Canyon and part of the ruins today
Source: *Chaco Culture National Historical Park, National Park Service (United States). No claim to original U.S. Government works.*

of these ancient village sites and cared for their communities portray the value of connection in learning and what happens to the learning process when the motivation is coming from a belief in or commitment to something greater than the individual. In particular, the construction of homes and adobe ovens for cooking, the planting, the harvesting, and the art were intergenerational activities where youth were mentored and apprenticed by their families and elders. The descendants of the people that lived in Chaco Canyon now reside in the Pueblos of New Mexico and the Hopi and Navajo reservations in Arizona and New Mexico. You can follow the family lines of contemporary artists whose elders were recognized in the White House during their lifetimes and by the National Endowment for the Arts for their superlative craft, such as Maria Martinez and Julian Martinez, who revived the blackware pottery, and Margaret Tafoya, who was known as the matriarch of the Santa Clara Pueblo potters. To experience learning like this, one must have a developed sense of empathy and compassion for oneself and others and the ability to engage in perspective-taking, to see a moment from another's point of view. These skills and dispositions are ingredients for being a good teammate. This chapter is about helping your students develop those skills and mindsets.

A recent study examined how young children's individual engagement with their teachers, their classmates, and their classroom work related to their learning readiness (Sabol et al., 2018). The study sample included 211 predominately low-income, racially and ethnically diverse 4-year-old children from 49 preschool classrooms in an unspecified medium-sized city in the United States. The study's outcomes showed that positive engagement enhanced children's learning readiness across the board. Good engagement with their teachers improved student's developing literacy skills. Positive engagement with their classmates improved language skills and self-regulation capacity. Conversely, children who had trouble engaging in the classroom experienced lower language, literacy, and self-regulatory skills and more conflict with teachers. These findings show us that the impetus to get along extends beyond socialization to achievement. Connection is important to the learning process on many levels.

Strategies to Develop Connection: An Overview

Connection Strategy 1:
Try a novel strategy called The Reverse Quiz to
promote collaboration among students.
This activity functions similarly to a flipped classroom (Berrett, 2012) and requires students to engage with each other in teams and then, as a larger group, to co-construct their understanding of content, evaluate and prioritize the content in order to present the most salient principles, and strengthen their presentation skills and ability to defend their positions and responses.

Connection Strategy 2:
Protect–Check–Inspect

Use the words "protecting," "checking," and "inspecting" as a simple way to pivot students into group work and to identify when you need to circle back to support individual students having trouble engaging with the group.

Connection Strategy 3:
Use reading instruction to help students explore imagination and develop an understanding of respect, compassion, and empathy.

Any teacher of literature, whether in elementary school or high school, will be familiar with the power of reading to help students understand and explore their emotional responses and to develop empathy for characters. While this is a longstanding feature of reading instruction, new neuroscience provides insight into the reasons why reading can be a powerful vehicle for the development of empathy and compassion.

Connection Strategy 4:
Almonds and Cherries

Disrupt stress and anxiety with a visualization strategy that uses almonds and cherries as a metaphor for the parts of the brain that produce stress chemistry and motivational reward chemistry.

Connection Strategy 5:
Positive Parody

Have kids to transform the lyrics of any song into an anthem of empowerment and joy, thus affirming prosocial messages about learning and achievement.

Connection in Action: A Portrait

A living example of exceptional teamwork among children can be found in the Lightning Boy Foundation Hoop Dancers, an intertribal group of children from Santa Fe, New Mexico. They are exceptional because of the support, sportsmanship, teamwork, and friendship they demonstrate across their age range, from 2.5 to 19 years old, as they train together and compete with one another. These young people hail from the American Indian Pueblos of Pojoaque, Nambé, Santa Clara, San Ildefonso, and the Hopi, Assinaboine, Mohawk, and Navajo nations. Several of these young dancers have captured world titles. A charismatic young boy whose life is the inspiration for this group, Valentino Tzigiwhaeno Rivera (Tino), danced his heart out during his short lifetime; Tzigiwhaeno means "lightning" in the Tewa language, which is spoken by the people of Pojoaque Pueblo. When he was alive, Tino's energy expanded vibrantly in all directions. When he passed away, his mother, Felicia Rosacker-Rivera, founded the Lightning Boy Foundation, dedicated to the mission of "nurturing confidence and integrity through culture and artistic expression" (lightningboyfoundation.com). Even in the throes of suffering from a severe brain and spinal cord injury he sustained in a car accident, Tino participated in his life and hoop dancing as fully as he was able, coaching his dancemates from his wheelchair and correcting their steps, pace, and attention to the drum beat and the songs.

Tino's life is permanently memorialized for the public in the form of a bronze sculpture that captures him in a vibrant, taut, ecstatic moment of

FIGURE 3.2: "Lightning Boy" bronze statue by George Rivera, Museum of Indian Arts and Culture, Santa Fe, New Mexico
Source: *George Rivera/georgeriverastudio.com*

hoop dancing. The sculpture was fashioned by his father, sculptor George Rivera, and graces the open plaza of the Museum of Indian Arts and Culture in Santa Fe, New Mexico (see Figure 3.2).

When Tino passed, it galvanized this group of children and their families to form a troupe committed to the hoop dance, which has its origins as a healing dance, and to share it with others. Many of the teenage members of the troupe danced as children alongside Tino. Because hoop dancing competition separates people by age but not gender, the boys and girls compete with each other in formal settings, all the while encouraging each other, coaching each other, and comforting each other. What if your classroom was as collaborative as this troupe of children?

What We Misunderstand About Connection and Teamwork

One of my favorite books about working as a team is an allegory called *Together is Better: A Little Book of Inspiration* by Simon Sinek (2016). Near the opening, Sinek says, "Leadership is not about being in charge, it's about taking care of those in your charge." What happens when a person is motivated to learn and perform in the service of something outside themselves, greater than themselves? Psychology researchers call the deeper factors that contribute to great teamwork the ABC's: attitudes, behaviors, and cognitive states (Weir, 2018). Taskwork is what gets done to complete an assignment and meet a goal. Teamwork consists of the behaviors, the feelings, and the contributions from each person to the team. How well these elements fit with each other can determine the quality of the team experience. And *how* a team works makes all the difference.

Team Structure Matters
One of the things we misunderstand about connection is that the team's structure—not just its existence—matters, and that it can either burden or liberate the thinking of members on that team. Salas et al. (2005) define the coordinating elements necessary for good teams:

1. shared mental models to anticipate and predict each other's needs and roles to meet the team's goal,
2. managing each other's differences in listening, processing speed,

working memory, communication style, and stress in order to meet
the team's goal, and

3. mutual trust, because "without sufficient trust, team members will expend their time and energy protecting, checking, and inspecting each other as opposed to collaborating to provide value-added ideas" (Salas et al., 2005, p. 568)

Neuroscience shows us that the brain finds fairness and cooperation rewarding (Tabibnia & Lieberman, 2007). Children pick up on inequities and imbalances of power from as young as 3 years old for verbal exchanges and as young as 8 months old for behavioral inconsistencies and nonverbal cues (Gülgöz & Gelman, 2017). Furthermore, people perform better when they are a part of network of like-minded collaborators than they do when there is a pecking order or a hierarchy (see Figure 3.3). My lab explored the influence that the team structures of networks (picture a web) and hierarchies (picture a tower) have on problem solving. We used a game, much like the popular board game Clue, that challenged players to figure out the who, what, where, when, why, and how of plans for a terrorist attack in order to make a plan to thwart it (Roberts, 2014). One team played in a hierarchy, where they had to send information up a chain of command, and the other team played in a network, where they could communicate information directly among themselves. As expected, the networked teams worked faster and more accurately than the hierarchical teams due to their ability to access and support each other's thinking.

People are faster and more accurate problem solvers when they work as a team in a network structure. Each person in the network has knowledge or skill that contributes to the overall solution, and one mind doesn't have to manage the load of the challenge alone.

The game challenged team players to use their working memory (to hold in mind and work with multiple pieces of information) and reasoning skills (to discern and determine the correct information). When these teams played while being observed by functional magnetic resonance imaging (fMRI), we observed a key difference between the two teamwork models. The players from both teams used the frontal lobes, which is where working memory and reasoning skills are supported in the brain. But the hierarchy team relied more heavily on working memory to

Tower

Teammates are isolated from each
other during problem solving, so each
brain has to work hard on its own.

Web

Teammates stay connected with each
other during problem solving, so one
brain doesn't tackle the problem alone.

FIGURE 3.3: Brains Work More Efficiently in Networks

problem solve, which meant that their brains were working hard on the demands, or the cognitive load, of the problem and also on monitoring their position in the hierarchy. The network team showed activation in a different part of the brain, one that helps a person monitor themselves within a task (Chang et al., 2019; Supekar & Menon, 2012; Craig, 2009). In short, the people working in the network team structure were able to be more flexible and accurate problem solvers. Cutting out the middleman resulted in more efficient and fluid problem solving.

Social Brains Operate Differently Than Those Who Spectate or Observe

Another important thing to understand about connection is that our brains function differently when we are being social than they do when we merely spectate or observe. Think of the differences in learning during complex instruction when one student dominates during group work and other students, typically the ones with special needs or second language challenges, stand passively to the side and watch. Some hyperscanning studies have mapped what the connection between two people actually looks like by measuring brain activity and timing between one person, who was the sender, and another, who was the receiver. These studies have enabled researchers to see what storytelling, gesturing, identifying facial expressions in order to grasp the other's emotions, and deciphering information about an intention from the sender looks like in the brains of both participants! Some of these studies have looked at musicians playing guitar duets (Sänger et al., 2012; Lindenberger et al., 2009) and at romantic couples because both are in tune with and sensitive to another's feelings and communication styles. In particular, the storytelling experiments illustrate that patterns of brain activity in the storyteller's brain and in the listener's brain are aligned with and share a similar pattern of activation (Stephens et al., 2010).

Teacher–Student Relationships Determine Learning Quality

Another study—one that has particular relevance in light of the emergency shift to remote learning during the COVID-19 pandemic—showed the differences between activity in the brain when someone is participating live with a person versus brain activity when watching a video of the person (Redcay et al., 2010). The live interactions activated brain regions that support social cognition and provide a feeling of reward. I call these the "good neurologies" because that social connection causes the release of prosocial neurochemistry that includes oxytocin, which bonds us to a person or a group, and dopamine, the reward chemical that gives us the motivational pull we feel toward something, someplace, or someone. Repeating the same social interaction using video activated additional parts of the brain that we use to keep an eye out for conflict and threat—one being part of the brain that breaks ties and helps you with yes/no, stop/go, and A versus B type choices, and also the amygdala, which is sensitive to negativity. In other words, learning online inserts an extra step the brain must contend with in order to settle into learning. That is, having to communicate through an online platform, even if you and your students already know and are comfortable with one another, still requires you to suppress or take the time to incorporate that monitoring step. For instance, you might be thinking and checking on things such as whether you or your screen are visible or whether you can see everyone else and follow what's happening through the computer screen so that you can socially connect.

However, whether learning occurs in person or on video is not the sole factor in the quality of learning; being in the classroom setting, alone, is not enough for a student to be able to learn. The group brain dynamic is a neuroscience method that captures the brain activity of more than two people at once and is being pioneered in classrooms as a way to map out learning quality among a group of students and their teacher. Bevilacqua et al. (2019) used wireless electroencephalography (EEG) to collect data from 12 senior high school students and their teacher during biology class. Six classroom sessions over the course of the term were organized that included content delivered to all 12 students in two different formats: video (teacher curated educational videos that aligned with her content) and live lecture (teacher delivered some content in live lecture format). At the end of each session, students were assessed with a 20-question multiple-choice quiz that included content from both delivery formats. The results? First, the students' retention of the lesson (measured by quiz scores) and brain-to-brain synchrony (measured by EEG) was stronger for video content than for the in-classroom lectures across the six classes. The research team surmised that because videos have such rich visual and auditory stimulation that students' attention was more entrained during videos than for lectures. Second, during the in-class lecture, only those students who reported greater social closeness to their teacher showed higher brain-to-brain synchrony with the teacher, and also the best retention of the content regardless of the presentation format. Finally, students reported engagement ratings each day of class. The engagement ratings predicted their synchrony to the teacher, not to their peers. The implication from this study is that the quality of the relationship with the teacher mattered to the point that if the relationship was strong enough, it didn't matter if the delivery was a lecture or an educationally-relevant video, because the index of student–teacher closeness correlated most closely with high quiz scores regardless of whether the quiz was from the lecture or the video. This study also found that the better the student's rating of their teacher, the smaller the differences in their brain synchrony between lecture and video. In this case, the student's relationship with their teacher was a stronger predictor of their engagement than their social connection to their peers.

One of the implications of this study is that a good relationship with the teacher inoculates students against situational motivation (liking one format or activity better than another) and leads to better retention of lesson content. This is encouraging in light of the constraints on the delivery of instruction using remote learning. If these findings bear out as this line of study broadens, the learning sciences are beginning to show us how entrainment can optimize attention during learning, and how social learning facilitates engagement and provides a protective buffer from attention that may wax and wane according to individual preference and interest. When you have days when you wonder if you make a difference, remember this study!

Teachers have significant emotional influence over students. Because of the number of months of the year, days of the week, and hours of the day that students spend in school, teachers are "significant others" in their students' lives. Evidence from hyperscanning studies illustrate how our brains can be influenced and entrained by people we are in significant relationship with (i.e., partner, family member, friend, teacher, coach, or mentor), and the studies literally give us a picture of what happens when two people engage with each other. Students anticipate and expect a lot from teachers every day. This body of research points to how important it is that the relationship be a great one.

I offer you five strategies that can help strengthen that relationship and help elevate your students' learning with connection to something greater outside of themselves.

An Educator's Experiments

The following experiments are based on learning strategies that were devised for groups ranging in age from kindergartners to adults, but can be adapted for students at multiple levels of schooling.

Connection Strategy 1:
Reverse Quiz—a combination of two proven teaching strategies: Jigsaw method and Socratic seminar.
One of the most important principles of differentiation is to devise meaningful work for your students that will advance some aspect of their skill or understanding. Reverse Quiz is a strategy I devised for my students at Northern New Mexico College (NNMC) that can be adapted for middle and high school as well as college students. I wanted to address equity and individual differences among the students I teach at NNMC, which sits a half hour north of Santa Fe and east of Los Alamos in Rio Arriba County,

New Mexico. In 2016, the county exceeded the average state percentages for children at or below the poverty level. My class rosters include students who all speak English, either as a first or a second language, and also speak Spanish, Filipino, Tewa, Apache, Keres, or Navajo. Many of the students who attend college at NNMC are already teachers who are working to support their families. Some are first-generation college students. Making their time in school count is my priority, because I know that family, cultural, and work responsibilities consume a lot of their time and energy.

Science Behind the Strategy

TEAMWORK AND RAPPORT. The jigsaw method (Aronson & Bridgeman, 1979), pioneered by Elliot Aronson and his students at the University of Texas at Austin in 1971, has a 50-year history for reducing racial tension in the classroom, reducing absenteeism, improving test performance, and increasing morale. It was originally developed to address learning inequities among students in communities at-risk. Furthermore, jigsaw has been shown to neutralize the differences among all students—those who may tend to dominate the group (fast), those who require more time (reflective), those who bore easily, and those who are more competitive—in favor of working as a team to further learning. Here are the basic steps of the jigsaw method:

1. Divide students into groups (vary students in the group by gender, ethnicity, race, and ability, or allow teams to self-select).
2. Appoint a leader or have the group select one.
3. Divide the content of the lesson between the groups, such as delegating one chapter per group.
4. You may elect to assign specific content to each student within a group. For instance, one group's chapter may have several key concepts and you may want to assign a specific lead to a certain concept, giving quieter students practice with presenting and reflective students a task they can focus on and prepare.
5. Give each group time to become the experts on their chapter, subject matter, or part of the lesson.
6. Form temporary expert groups in which one person from each expert group now joins an expert from each of the other groups.

They discuss main points and prepare to bring the new information back to their original group.

7. Bring students back to original their jigsaw group to debrief.
8. Circulate among groups in order to listen and intervene if a student is too dominant or disruptive.
9. Model how to address those problems and correct the social balance.
10. Students take a quiz on the material at the end.

(From https://www.jigsaw.org/#steps)

Socratic seminar is a strategy that helps students understand ideas, issues, and values associated with their content through group discussion (Paraskevas & Wickens, 2003; Adler, 1982). This strategy promotes active listening and perspective-taking. One of the most helpful aspects of the method is to develop rules of engagement for the class, such as: referring to evidence from the text to support your ideas, paraphrasing what others say to check your understanding, and learning to offer alternative interpretations without putting down ideas of other participants. (See more at https://www.facinghistory.org/resource-library/teaching-strategies/socratic-seminar)

The Reverse Quiz, a combination of these two methods, requires each student to engage with a team of three or four of their classmates and choose four or five core questions that represent the key takeaways from one chapter of their reading. I ask the team to choose wisely because their absent classmates will take this quiz as a make-up assignment. They are not just working for themselves, but also supporting classmates who were unable to attend that session. Each team scribes their questions and answers on the board or types them into a word document to show on a Smartboard. I, in turn, begin to probe their understanding more deeply by engaging them in a Socratic seminar so that they can respond to me and to each other and elaborate beyond the core questions they generated from each chapter.

I have found that this is a strong way to promote equity and trust among my students whose lives and schedules require them to respond to demands that compete with their study time. Instead of coming to class worried about not keeping up or being ill-prepared for a traditional drill quiz, they team up and support each other as they actively mine the core content from their reading together. Then, we animate that content as a class in a way that draws their interest, promotes their understanding, and allows them to form teams and have each other's backs instead of feeling performance anxiety. Whether a student finished their reading or understood everything becomes less consequential because those gaps will be filled in by the Reverse Quiz process. Students leave with a stronger grasp of the content, having worked with each other, listened to personal experiences, and defended their positions and opinions with information from the reading. Furthermore, once they realize that they can support each other, learn from each other's experience, and understand that I am going to engage them in rigorous but supportive questioning that is designed to be fun, comfortable, and thought-provoking, they relax and improve with every quiz session. What used to be an exercise in dread turns into a class they look forward to coming to. The result? I get fewer emails apologizing for not being prepared, about missing an assignment, or asking for more time to complete coursework. Class attendance ceases to be a problem. Most importantly, their mindsets have shifted from being anxious about balancing life with school to anticipating a class session that will energize and refresh them and connect them to their own learning and each other.

Connection Strategy 2:
Use a play on the words "protecting," "checking," and "inspecting" from Salas et al. (2005) to (1) detect and redirect your students when trust issues emerge during group work, and (2) help a student transition from self-interest to giving their attention and motivation to the group.
You may think that assigning students with complimentary skill sets to teams or even letting them select their own membership will promote good teamwork and collaboration. But dispositions and mindsets differ among students as surely as individual differences in their working memory and processing speed. Neuroscience shows us that different systems of reasoning and problem solving appear depending whether a person views themselves and their role as with or outside of their team (Le Bouc & Pessiglione, 2013; De Waal, 2008). On the surface they may appear involved, but the quality of their thinking is determined by how they view their status in the group (see Table 3.1).

TABLE 3.1: A matrix of research from neuroscience and social science to help you shape a team mindset in your classroom and intervene when teams or certain individuals need more support.

	Students having trouble with team membership Have a Focus on Self	Students in a healthy team relationship Pay Attention to Others
Brain Activity (Le Bouc & Pessiglione, 2013)	Brain regions that are devoted to seeking rewards for individual gain become active	Brain regions that are devoted to social cognition and connection become active
Behavior (De Waal, 2008)	Work from a place of self-centeredness and ego	Work from a place of altruism
Classroom Heuristic: Protect, Check, Inspect (Salas et al., 2005)	A person wants to protect themselves from a group or within a group	A person engages and participates comfortably in a group
Protect	Protect yourself	Protect others—have each other's backs
Check	Keep a check on yourself to avoid criticism or attention	Keep a check on how others are functioning in their roles; model how to give constructive feedback
Inspect	Watch for and call out others who are not contributing to the team	Inspect your own performance in the spirit of collaboration and working for the greater goal at hand

Using Table 3.1 to guide your students in teams, use the catchphrase "Protect–Check–Inspect" to discern when your students need modeling or coaching to be fully present and collaborative:

PROTECT: Are they more interested in protecting themselves or do they have each other's backs? If they are not working as a team, have a conversation about how much more energy they would have if they were collectively watching out for each other instead of the back and forth of comparing themselves to the whole. This hearkens back to the finding that networked teams operate more efficiently.

CHECK: Is someone in the group self-conscious and trying to avoid criticism, or are they all supporting their teammates? This is a good time to model how to give constructive feedback in a way that isn't personal. For instance, students have to give a positive and a supportive suggestion together, so the recipient knows they are coming from a point of appreciation and improving the circumstance for everyone.

INSPECT: This step is the inverse of Check. Is someone in the group watching to call out others who are not being good citizens on the team? Encourage that student to inspect their own contributions and identify and articulate the ways that they are supporting the collective goal.

Science Behind the Strategy

POSITIVE EMOTIONS GROUND AND BROADEN THINKING. Fredrickson's broaden-and-build theory of positive emotions starts from the premise that positive emotions broaden and open the mind. Her work has collated numerous studies over two decades to illustrate that emotions such as anger and fear close the mind, while emotions such as contentment and joy open or broaden the mind (Fredrickson, 2004). Indeed, one of her initial experiments involved testing the effectiveness of positive emotion to undo the effects of negative emotion. The finding? The heart rates of people exposed to negative emotion took up to one minute to recover, while the heart rates of people exposed to positive emotion took only 20 seconds to return to a resting baseline. She has since replicated this finding across age, gender, and ethnicity (Fredricksen, 2013). Behavioral and neuroimaging studies show the anatomical basis of this effect, illustrating the relationship between mood states and changes in the way the brain accesses and uses visual attention and control on cognitive and creative tasks (Garland et al., 2010; Schmitz et al., 2009; Rowe et al., 2007). The Protect-Check-Inspect strategy is a simple incarnation of this idea that can give you a quick way to assess how your students are doing among each other and also language you can use to help students pivot from self to team.

Connection Strategy 3:
Use reading instruction to explore imagination and develop an understanding of respect, compassion, and empathy. In short, help children understand that everyone needs a do-over sometimes, a chance to do better.

Aaliya Casados and Kathleen Gentry, two undergraduate students from my Teaching and Diagnosis of Reading course at NNMC in Spring 2019, developed a lesson based on the popular children's book *Where the Wild Things Are*, by Maurice Sendak (1963). They enlisted the imaginations of their kindergarten students through reading the book and watching the film adaptation to experience sympathy for and then empathy with Max, the book's main character. Through their understanding of the story, students have a chance to relate to Max, to create a new Wild Thing that portrays their impressions and feelings, and to engage in the story with their parents, caregiver, or other family member, classmates and teachers to engage in a lesson about behavior, trust, love, and second chances. A great resource for books that begin these kinds of conversations is Nancy Boyles's *Classroom Reading to Engage the Heart and Mind: 200+ Picture Books to Start SEL Conversations* (2020).

Science Behind the Strategy
EMPATHY, COMPASSION, AND CONNECTION. Empathy and compassion can be cultivated (Cotton, 1992). So can kindness (Mascaro, Darcher, Negi & Raison, 2015; Galante, Galante, Bekkers, & Gallacher, 2014), beginning as early as preschool years (Flook, Goldberg, Pinger, & Davidson, 2015). Encouraging children to discuss their feelings and problems and reasoning with children, even very young ones, about how their behavior can affect others, and why it is important to share and be kind, has been shown to promote empathy and prosocial behavior (Clarke, 1984). Furthermore, reading fiction promotes empathy (Mar et al., 2009). The formula for a good story lies in its dramatic arc, which includes a beginning based on something surprising or novel happening that unfolds in such a way that the main character has to contend with an obstacle or crisis that most likely involved something from their past, and then come to terms with it in order to experience transformation. The term for that effect, transportation, means the

point when you begin to emotionally empathize with a story's characters. This is the point where stories become social (Zak, 2013). And when social connection happens in a positive way, such as when someone feels trust, compassion, or generosity, the brain releases oxytocin. Also known as the love hormone, oxytocin is a chemical part of our neurology that provides social glue and bonds us to our mates and families (Olff et al., 2013) and contributes to that feeling of well-being in a group (Stallen et al., 2012). One study illustrated that transportation is what influences how well fiction promotes empathy (Bal & Veltkamp, 2013). Without it, the link between empathy and fiction reading was not found.

Empathy also has a relationship with overall academic achievement. In a meta-analysis looking at the effectiveness of 213 school-based universal social and emotional learning (SEL) programs, over 270,000 children from kindergarten through high school were evaluated to show an 11-percentile-point gain in achievement when they were compared to children who did not participate in the program (Durlak et al., 2011). This relationship has also been demonstrated in a smaller study that measured empathy in 8- and 9-year-old girls and its influence on their reading and spelling skills at ages 10 and 11 (Feshbach & Feshbach, 2009).

Connection Strategy 4:
Try instilling a simple habit, called Almonds and
Cherries, to help control stress and anxiety.

I devised this strategy while working with military veterans recovering from post-traumatic stress disorder and have also used it to coach middle schoolers, gifted children dealing with perfectionism, college students, and with children, adults, and families in my practice to help people of all ages reframe how they view stress and anxiety. Almonds and Cherries represent the brain's similarly shaped amygdala (almond), which processes negative stress, and the nucleus accumbens (cherries), which process reward and motivation (see Figure 3.4). A quick way to experience the action of the nucleus accumbens is to open social media, FaceTime, or a shopping app on your smartphone. The gratification you feel in that moment and the urge to do it again comes from the squirt of dopamine the nucleus accumbens just gave your brain.

Figure 3.4. Almonds (negative emotion) and cherries (positive emotion)

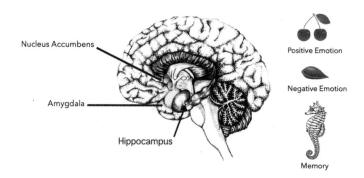

FIGURE 3.4: Visualization can help you disrupt negative emotion

correspond to and are an analogy for the relationship of the amygdala to the nucleus accumbens, two structures that influence memory through their neurochemistry, which promote stress or provide a feeling of incentive, motivation and reward.

You can use almonds and cherries for this exercise or ask your students to imagine them. First, put, or ask students to imagine, an almond (or a bean, if nut allergies are an issue) in their hand. Keep or have them imagine one in yours and ask them to look at the real or imagined almond in their hand. Ask them to close their hand around it, and open their hand, and close their hand around it, and open their hand. Once they've done that three times, say to them, "The piece of your brain that makes you feel afraid, worried, stressed, or overwhelmed is the size of what you're holding in your hand. It's not bigger than you, even though it feels like it might be. You can hold that piece in the palm of your hand that determines whether something is interesting to you or stressful to you. And so, the next time that you feel afraid, stressed, or confused, remember this moment, look at your hand, and imagine the almond in the palm of your hand. Open your hand and close it, open your hand and close it, and tell yourself, 'I've got this. I'm bigger than this piece of myself. Using my whole mind and body, I can overcome this moment.'" Next, put two cherries (or grapes) in the palm of their other hand, or ask them to imagine them there, and remind them that the piece of their brain that makes them feel excited about something, eager to learn something, or eager to have something, is about the size of these two cherries that they are holding in their hand. Ask them what they notice about these two cherries when they compare them to the almond. They're going to notice (1) that the cherries are bigger than the almond, and (2) that there is a 2:1 ratio between the cherries and the almond. The piece of their brain that makes them feel stressed is small compared to the whole. The part of the brain that supports your curiosity, pleasure, and sense of discovery is bigger than the part of the brain that causes you stress. There are twice as many cherries as there are almonds, and they are bigger than that small stress organ.

Use this exercise to develop a mindset (habit) and a shorthand that gives you a common context and reference point to help students reduce their stress in a way that doesn't derail your lesson. The other benefit of this strategy is that, over time, you can enlist students to help each other when they become stressed. You build their capacity to understand their own relationship with fear, stress, and challenge. You also promote an environment that is prosocial, where students develop empathy to support each other in their learning. Over time, students become less dependent on you and more supportive of each other, checking in on each other, having each other's backs like a good team. The hypothesized outcome for this is that you're going to have students who—no matter how they come in the door in the morning, how they come into your class, nor the time of the day—will enter into a state of mind and rapport with each other that's going to be learning friendly. It doesn't take away all of the individual things that could be happening in their lives, but it does set an expectation of how they're going to be for themselves and with each other when they are with you. See if this doesn't improve the quality of on-task time and their willingness to take risks in their learning—the parts of the brain that help you feel motivated to learn also influence risk-taking.

Science Behind the Strategy
THE SAME PARTS OF THE BRAIN CAN FUEL POSITIVE OR NEGATIVE LEARNING, DEPENDING ON THE CONTEXT. The frontal lobes are set up for higher-level thinking skills, such as supporting your ability to plan, anticipate, perceive difficulty, multitask, and handle unexpected events. The seat, or bottom, of the frontal lobes are where emotions and uncertainty are processed (Nassar et al., 2019; Kalbfleisch et al., 2007). The nuclei accumbens and amygdalae (you have one of each in your left and right

hemispheres) are nestled in this area that borders the hippocampus, the "docking station" and "zip drive" of memory. The amygdala sends signals to the adrenal glands that release the flood of adrenaline that influences whether the hippocampus serves, promotes, and stores memory during a condition of optimal stress and learning readiness, or inhibits it because levels of anxiety are too high. Not far from the amygdalae, you have another set of nuclei called the nucleus accumbens, which are made up of two parts, the core and the shell. They're fueled by dopamine, the reward chemical, which is released when you're excited, incentivized, and motivated (Reynolds & Berridge, 2008; Abler et al., 2006). The interesting thing about the nucleus accumbens is that its function is highly influenced by context and it can also be involved in a stress response. For example, a study by Reynolds and Berridge (2008) was performed on rats but has a generalizable observation for humans: They observed that when the rats were in their home environment, the percentage of neurons supporting appetite (positive motivation) were prevalent across the nucleus accumbens. When the rats were outside their home, the neural activation pattern included a mix of neurons for appetite and neurons that were ambivalent, that is, they alternated between positive (the animals demonstrated appetite) and negative (the animals demonstrated fear) input. When the rats were placed in a stressful environment outside of their home, the percentage of neurons tuned for appetite diminished and became only a small subset of the whole, now outnumbered by neurons poised to code uncertain and stressful information. It isn't that the number of neurons changed in nucleus accumbens. Instead, each carried the potential to be used in a motivation response for food or a fear response. Depending on where the neurons were located within the nucleus accumbens and the environment the animal was in (home, out of their home, or exposed to stressful conditions), each would fire to facilitate appetite or promote fear, and the percentage of neurons devoted to either state changed based on the environment. Context matters!

ONE SENSE (VISION) CAN OVERRIDE ANOTHER (PAIN). This strategy marries the sensation of holding almonds or cherries and opening and closing the hand several times with the visualization and affirmation that students can override their anxiety. It is well-established that the neuroplasticity of our senses can be used to promote healing (Ramachandran & Rogers-Ramachandran, 2000). Pioneering research on phantom limb syndrome provides the dramatic example of a man relieved of the pain that caused his depression and anxiety. The man lost his arm in a motorcycle accident but still experienced the feeling of gripping pain in his lost arm for nearly a decade (Ramachadran & Hirstein, 1998). Dr. Ramachandran had the idea to construct a wooden box with a mirror positioned in such a way that when the man put his existing hand and arm into the box, the mirror made it look like he had both limbs! The healing moment came when Dr. Ramachandran asked him to open and close his hand. As the man did that, the pain of his phantom limb subsided. Visual imagery is a tool that is prevalently used in clinical settings for healing (Pearson, 2019; Pearson et al., 2015). A picture is worth a thousand words. Cognitive science shows us that our mind can grasp an image so powerfully that it conflates it to be something real, an effect that goes beyond words (Mathews et al., 2013). By seeing or visualizing the size of those brain structures (amygdala and nucleus accumbens), the person realizes their whole self is literally bigger and more than those parts, which inspires their confidence and resolve to overcome the anxiety of that moment.

Connection Strategy 5:
Positive Parody
Bryan Eason, a musician, activist and teacher from Mesquite, Texas, teaches classroom teachers to take children through a process that involves substituting negative lyrics from pop music with more positive ones. Most children like the beat and sound of pop music, but the lyrics may leave you wanting to turn off the song. This program allows you to keep the song, love the song, but change the lyrics. Teachers and children re-write the lyrics to turn them into joyful songs that encourage and reinforce learning skills. Note that although Bryan calls his strategy "Positive Parody," there is an important distinction to be made between true parody, publication of which is generally defensible as "fair use" of copyrighted material, and satire, unauthorized publication of which may be copyright infringement. These pieces probably fall into the latter category. So although the exercise is most likely fine for in-class use, students' work should not be shared online on YouTube, for example, or in any other public forum.

Science Behind the Strategy

RHYTHM, MUSIC, AND ENTRAINMENT. As covered in Chapter 1, rhythm can entrain the bodily systems that forge an emotional connection and release the reward and pleasure neurotransmitter dopamine. That good neurology emotionally "stamps" or reinforces learning. The chemical double whammy lies in the fact that music is social and promotes a process (the release of oxytocin) that unfolds like a string of pearls to spring music-evoked emotion (Chanda & Levitin, 2013). In fact, this is the basis for the chills you get when you hear a powerful piece of music (Koelsch et al., 2006). Koelsch (2010) calls these functions of music the Seven Cs:

1. Contact: prevents social isolation
2. Cognition: elicits aspects of social cognition, such as empathy, kindness, and connection
3. Co-pathy: brings individuals from separate pages onto the "same sheet of music," individual mind states center on the shared experience (e.g., calms one person's anxiety, evokes happy memories in another's mind and heart)
4. Communication: promotes self-regulation (e.g., a mother soothing her baby with a lullaby or a teacher using rhythm to relax and entrain the attention of their students)
5. Coordination: brings a listener in tune with their natural musical state (i.e., do they naturally synchronize or feel more comfortable with their own drumbeat)
6. Cooperation: promotes a desire to share an experience
7. Cohesion: fulfills the human need to belong, promotes confidence in reciprocity and trust, and creates what Trehub (2003) calls a moment of "oxytocin-mediated dissolution and restructuring of interpersonal boundaries" (p. 672)

There is also a reciprocity between music, lyrics, and language. Across psychology and neuroscience literatures, there is mounting evidence that musical skill has positive transfer effects to general and specific skills such as phonological awareness, naming speed, spelling, vocabulary, reading comprehension, speech perception, and attentional control (Slater et al.,

2015; Carr et al., 2014; Tierney et al., 2013a, White et al., 2013). This strategy marries and co-opts these features of language learning in the service of creating motivating song lyrics to popular tunes.

Neuromyth Checkpoint: Assumptions to Question

Assumption 1:
Hierarchies are bad for learning.

Hierarchies serve a purpose and are necessary to promote social structure for certain situations. Sometimes it isn't possible to have a team that functions in a horizontal orientation. Leadership implies that that there is a superior who maintains, monitors, and organizes group activity. School leadership teams are often hierarchical. The insight that a hierarchical structure can impose extra burden on working memory shows us that one of the responsibilities of a superior is to monitor team activity to make sure no one becomes overwhelmed. If there is a build-up of burden on working memory, the superior can intervene and re-delegate aspects of the task to other people on the team so that the overall team is successful. On the other hand, teachers can capitalize on the network format to enhance student's collaboration and intellectual performance.

Assumption 2:
Constructing the team automatically leads to powerful group learning.

Teams can be perfectly constructed, but in order to be successful, they need authentic problems with enough depth and complexity that all involved can legitimately contribute to the outcome. Two examples of powerful team learning include anchored instruction and problem-based learning. Anchored instruction is based on video stories created so that they can be mined for information and interacted with in order to represent true and real problem solving (Bransford et al., 1990). Problem-based learning is another strategy that promotes team learning by focusing on rich meaningful problems. Originally pioneered in medical education, problem-based learning has been adopted to serve the needs of gifted students and as a framework to guide collaborative learning.

TAKEAWAYS FOR SMALL BUT POWERFUL CHANGES IN PRACTICE

➤ Teamwork and collaboration promote the neurochemistry of "good learning neurologies"—systems related to trust, empathy, anticipation, and reward.

➤ The quality of the relationship between a student and a teacher matters and touches motivation in a powerful way you might not expect.

➤ Modeling the mindsets and processes of trust and collaboration will inoculate your classroom against toxic stress.

➤ An individual's performance is best among a lateral network of teammates rather than in a hierarchy.

CHAPTER 4

Masking

I n the first three chapters, I talked about ways the classroom can support the development of flexibility, readiness, and connection. By now, you are learning that certain behaviors that appear irrelevant or counterproductive are actually ways that we are all wired in support of our learning. Human neuroimaging methods give us the opportunity to look below the surface of behaviors associated with learning. These techniques allow us to see what's happening inside the brain while we compare and contrast it to what a person is doing on the outside. For instance, children with high-functioning autism will perform on visual reasoning tasks as well as or better than their neurotypical peers (Sahyoun et al., 2010), but their brains use different regions to achieve the same goal (Brar et al., 2009). If we didn't have neuroimaging, we would assume that visual reasoning skills are not affected by autism because these kids perform the same or even better.

What we're learning, now that we have the ability to see activity in the brain with neuroimaging, is that its regions and systems are always partnering to adapt to the environmental context. Neurons in the resting state quiet down parts of the brain that are not needed for an active task. But the quiet is misleading, because important processing is happening in that system, too. For example, a brain area classically known to drive a process (such as calculating 2 + 2) will be involved, but depending on the social and emotional contexts, other areas will either support the process (in a motivational state) or diminish its effectiveness (in an anxious state). The brain is designed to respond to experience and feedback. Neuroplasticity helps the brain's processing to adjust, anticipate, and fit the environment. Therefore, different configurations of brain processing emerge from moment to moment. It isn't that our current knowledge of certain intellectual pathways and systems (such as for reading, math, or reasoning) of the brain is incorrect. It's that a basic skill region in the brain that reads, calculates, or reasons joins a larger connective network that gets called forth by the context of the learning environment—and whether that environment is comfortable or anxious, boring or engaging, makes a difference. One of the mantras in this book is that context matters! Now that you have liberated student learning by using methods to promote flexibility, readiness, and connection, the final piece to consider in your approach to differentiation is that context determines what shows up in the brain and whether strong learning is promoted. If you don't fit your learning context, things don't go well.

What is Masking?

The Cambridge English Dictionary describes masking as "preventing something from being seen or noticed." Masking describes the veil over suffering that teachers and students alike experience when the root cause of a student's behavior isn't obvious to the naked eye. Being misunderstood is one of the greatest causes of human suffering. And when it happens in a classroom, it can break the learning process. For instance, females are much more likely to be diagnosed with autism later in life or not at all because they develop social behaviors, such as the ability to give eye contact, that camouflage autism. A failure to diagnose autism can result in greater levels of stress, anxiety, and depression, and it impacts genders differently. This masking, or camouflaging caused by a failure to diagnose autism, has been shown to result in increased levels of depression in men with autism and increased states of vigilance or high alert stress in women with autism (Lai et al., 2017). Masking also happens when someone has abilities that cover for weaker skills. For example, highly able children with strong verbal skills can have a condition called stealth dyslexia (Eide & Eide, 2012), which is characterized by reading and writing performance that don't match ability, frustration with reading comprehension or, in some cases, competent comprehension but only able to get the gist of what they read because more basic language processes are not working properly. The problem with masking is that these kinds of students may achieve at appropriate levels for the purposes of classroom education, but unfortunately, they are achieving well below their ability level. The processes of learning to cross a mediocre finish line are fraught with stress for these types of learners. I see this among twice exceptional children (those who are both gifted and learning disabled) whose teachers say they are doing "fine" in the classroom, but whose parents will narrate the severe stress and anxiety that plague their family's evening hours during homework time.

Strategies to Get Behind the Mask: An Overview

Unmasking Strategy 1:
Get to the root of performance issues and executive functions.

Power struggles and misunderstandings occur when your impression of a student doesn't match what's really happening in their learning. You may have heard the popular mantra that what looks like "won't" in a student is most likely "can't." Look for the probable causes of behavior in their executive function capacities instead of responding to the behavior itself.

Unmasking Strategy 2:
Develop a learning contract with your students that will guide how you and they will respond to mistakes during learning.

This strategy shows you how to work with mistakes during learning and shape a healthy understanding of them and their importance in learning. Use this strategy to address perfectionism, learned helplessness, and a host of other behaviors that emerge when someone errs or misjudges their performance.

Unmasking Strategy 3:
Unmask threat, stress, and anxiety with analogy,
metaphor, and divergent thinking.
Diverting a student's attention away from stress and anxiety with a good puzzle or intriguing question can constructively restore mood and engagement.

Unmasking Strategy 4:
Add "for now" to the end of a student's description of their struggle to interrupt the flow of anxiety and bring their attention back to the present.
Both language and visualization techniques have proven to influence emotional processing (Pessoa et al., 2012; Lindquist et al., 2006; Davidson et al., 2000). This strategy, called For Now, is similar to Almonds and Cherries and is another way to teach your students to disrupt a moment of overwhelm, to restore composure, and, over time, to support mental health and well-being.

Unmasking Strategy 5:
Identify the lonely, disconnected, and bullied.
I didn't invent this strategy, but when I read it, I was compelled to share it here. It is a simple strategy for unmasking students who may be socially vulnerable and struggling under your radar.

Unmasking in Action: Two Portraits

Here are stories of two young people that illustrate masking in action.

Anya—Stealth Dyslexia
I was in a middle school classroom where a high-achieving student, Anya, a delight to her teachers, was beginning to refuse to go to school. In the mornings, her parents started to witness tears, anxiety, and inflexibility they didn't know she possessed. She earned excellent grades and got along well with her peers. To the naked eye, Anya appeared to be the model student. The day I was in her classroom, the teacher asked each student to open up their laptops to a mindfulness program the school uses to track

stress and performance anxiety. A sliding scale appeared on the screen. The left side was green, and the right side was red. Students were supposed to slide the bar either left (relaxed) or right (stressed). Anya pushed the bar all the way over to the right-hand side! But watching her, you wouldn't know she was having trouble. The culprit? Testing revealed a superior IQ and a case of stealth dyslexia. Anya is so bright and amenable; teachers couldn't see the problem. Her strong verbal skills masked her frustration and difficulty with reading comprehension (van Viersen et al., 2016). It looked like she learned effortlessly when, in reality, her homework was piling up faster than she could complete it, and she began to experience failure and self-esteem issues that she had no words to explain. Thus, the school refusal behavior. When I shared this moment in my observation with her team of teachers, they were amazed. Teachers thought they were seeing a high-achieving student with a pleasant demeanor. The stress indicator went unnoticed. Her teachers now know that because of an underlying auditory processing weakness, Anya may not remember all of the directions at once. My feedback was: "Here's what you think you see [a pleasant, high-achieving student], but this is what's really happening [she's expending a lot of energy compensating for her difficulties in class, so no one notices], and the next time Anya indicates high stress on the computer program, I want you to try A or B, and see if that doesn't lead to a different outcome." In this case, A was to approach Anya once the class gets started on independent or team work and ask if she understands the lesson, knows what to do next, and has the resources to begin, so that the teachers could situate her learning. In case her anxiety is related to something outside the classroom, I offered B, which in this case was to send her to get a drink of water or run an errand to a teacher down the hall so she can take a walk and get a stress break that will go unnoticed by her peers.

There were a few disconnects for Anya in the classroom. First, she shared the classroom with 31 other students. This level of noise and chaos overwhelmed Anya. But she wouldn't act out. Anya would try to follow along as best as she could, take a longer time with homework, and ask her peers to coach her understanding and fill her in on the side. Because the root of her dyslexia was trouble with an auditory processing disorder, every time she tried to focus on a specific part of the lesson, the rest of it would move past her. Her anxiety level would rocket in response. Anya's achievement in class wasn't suffering, but she was. Her homework sessions were major undertakings, as she would spend the evening reconstructing the entire lesson from the pieces she had focused on and the cues her classmates had given her instead of just completing the assigned practice piece. Anya was masking her own effort and struggle to achieve.

David—High-Functioning Autism

I was overseeing a month-long winter college arts program where students came to a camp to learn an art. A young man we'll call David was taking a silversmithing class. The studio held 12 people, so there were 2 teachers and 10 students. As you can imagine, it was a lively place, full of machinery—grinders, blow torches, saws, and polishers that make rough stone and silver gleam and shine as new jewelry. As students delved into the process of making jewelry, the room became noisy, dusty, and full of the smells of dust from grinding stone and propane. Students traded off using the speakers to plug in their iPods, sharing playlists while they worked. At the end of the first week, David became very flustered and upset when, not yet an expert with the tools, he couldn't get a stone to turn into what he wanted with the grinder. Alarmed, his teachers' first responses were to try to calm him down. In spite of their efforts, he became more hostile, raised his voice, and began to stim, flapping his arms. I heard about the episode at supper that evening. What his two teachers didn't realize was that David has autism. And what they were witnessing was sensory overload and difficulties with fine motor skill, two characteristics that are common features of autism. Luckily, David's college advisor was chaperoning students from his school and agreed to be his buddy for the rest of the class. The studio teachers set up a small workstation with some supplies for him in the foyer just outside the studio and close to the kitchen, where the class took afternoon tea breaks. His teachers encouraged him to adopt a collage approach, fitting rough-hewn stones into mosaic patterns, instead of trying to craft stones into fine jewelry to avoid upsetting the flow of the class and putting David's safety at risk from working with the cutting and grinding equipment. Everyone adjusted beautifully to this change, and they all enjoyed the weeks that followed. The real victory came when David opted to return again the next year to take pottery! Pottery is a gentler, more forgiving medium than silversmithing, and he was able to fully participate in the art. His second-year experience unfolded without a problem. He also came out of his shell and felt more confident about socializing, sharing information about his disability, and engaging with his classmates during outings.

What We Misunderstand About Masking

What we misunderstand about masking is the emotional toll it takes on students and their families, and the lost learning opportunity. As these effects accumulate over time, a person becomes less and less likely to realize their potential. This kind of stress can exacerbate mental illness and hopelessness in school-aged children, establishing a dangerous precedent for the unfolding of their adult lives and the health of their social, family, and personal relationships (Blaas, 2014; van Battenberg-Eddes & Jolles, 2013; Dyrda, 2009; Hinshaw, 1992). This is particularly worrisome because masking happens in many instances where students are quite capable but don't have an affinity for school. This mismatch results in a tremendous loss in our collective brain trust, as these issues that develop in school shape adult life in regretful ways. Both the individual and society lose out on the realization of intellectual and creative potential and the constructive contributions that could have emerged. Under-achievement is costly to the person's quality of life and mental health and also costly to society, as these individuals may require the support of social services, corrections, mental health, and other community systems later in life.

The other thing we misunderstand about masking has to do with bodily processes that help integrate learning on neural and sensory levels. I'd like to introduce and associate three body processes that influence how and how well someone learns: stress, low registration, and the hemodynamic BOLD response. These processes can all slow a person's response to what is being asked of them and to what is going on around them. Behaviorally, all three can look similar on the surface.

Stress and Low Registration

Stress, from mild to traumatic, alters someone's attention to their surroundings and influences their perception of what is happening around them (Cohen, Kamarck & Mermelstein, 1983). The Yerkes-Dodson, or inverted U-dose, response curve is a model of the relationship between emotional arousal and stress chemistry (Hanoch & Vitouch, 2004; Yerkes & Dodson, 1908). When your brain chemistry is on the left side of the inverted U (picture an upside-down U), stress is working for you, you feel ready and poised for action. When stress rises to the top of the U and tips over to the other side, stress becomes toxic, and its chemistry floods the hippocampus like a moat. What you know can't come out, and what's in store for you can't come in. Often, the discussion about learning and the hippocampus has to do with recalling memory or beginning the formation of new memories. But we are also learning that the hippocampus is a part of other neural systems that drive more subtle processes, those that are related to prediction and imagining novel events, envisioning, planning, decision making, and problem solving (Buckner, 2010; Madore, Szpunar, Addis & Schacter, 2016). There is a reason that plasticity in this part of the brain is so sensitive to the conditions of boredom and stress.

As far back as the 1940s, neuroscience research on rats showed that one of the physiological properties of the hippocampus is to reorganize and reorder events outside of the sequence in which they took place (Tolman, 1946). Later work in computational neuroscience outlined a process called *temporal compression* (Skaggs, McNaughton, Wilson & Barnes, 1996; August & Levy, 1999) that also occurs in the hippocampus. Temporal compression describes the capacity for the hippocampus to recall a sequence of cell firings at faster rates than they were first experienced. The key to this process is that once the learning has been experienced in real time, the nervous system can unpin the memory from real time and process the learned input at a faster rate. This occurs during a certain phase of sleep, defined by theta rhythm, one of the two prevalent brainwaves during sleep in the brain. The speed of temporal compression (how fast the hippocampus can replay a sequence of cell firings) is proportional to the activity level that took place during remembering and to the length of time engaged in learning, whether it was mental or physical. You could think of this process as the brain's zip drive unpacking experience and information at high speed. When the day's learning is done and you lie down to sleep, your brain moonlights to help you recover from the day's exertion and release what it no longer needs. These intrinsic properties of the hippocampus, and the fact that it is surrounded by parts of the brain that process emotion and reward (amygdala and nucleus accumbens, parts of the adrenalin- and dopamine-fueled systems), hint at where some of the neurological reciprocity lies between the resting state and effortful attention and cognition.

Low registration is a term used by the clinical community to characterize a person's failure to register sensory or emotional responses or reactions to an event in the moment it happens. People with low registration have difficulty getting motivated, often lag behind during group activity, and are prone to daydream. Consequently, you may see emotional reactions or behaviors in a student that don't match the moment or the context. These delayed behaviors typically take the form of outbursts or irritability (Engel-Yeger et al., 2016; Ludlow et al., 2014) and can be a symptom of post-traumatic stress, trauma, or disability such as autism (Smith et al., 2013; Dyregrov & Yule, 2006).

The BOLD Response: Sluggish Signaling in Our Brains

Finally, the way that we measure brain activity during functional MRI is based on a signal that reveals this sluggishness. Typically, images of the human brain from neuroscience studies show red, yellow, and orange spots, superimposed on a grayscale brain image, that indicate the part(s) of the brain that are involved in the task at hand. Those bright spots are called the blood oxygen level dependent, or BOLD, signal. The BOLD signal emerges in specific regions in the brain 3–16 seconds after the person takes action. To make this more concrete, let me illustrate a bit on this piece of our physiology. (You can use this to teach your students about this concept, too.) Our bodies are made of different tissues—muscle fiber, fat, skin, bone, cartilage, etc. Our brains are made of different tissues—gray matter, white matter, pia mater, glia, neurons, astrocytes, and oligodendrocytes, to name a few. Gray matter, white matter, cerebral spinal fluid, bone, and the soft tissues that encase the skull all have different densities. When the brain transmits information within the central nervous system or into the body through the spinal cord, that information travels at various rates. Imagine that you ask your students to count to 10 very slowly, one number per second. The metabolism in the parts of the brain that become active as they do that won't peak until after they're finished counting. Next, ask them to sit quietly after they count to 10. About 5–10 seconds after that, their brains will have reached that peak metabolism in the systems that helped them keep time and count to 10. What we think takes only 10 seconds to do in real time takes the brain's internal metabolism longer to execute, recover, and switch to the next demand.

Like hearing the roar of the crowd after everyone has already left the stadium, the experience of the nervous systems of your students is of you having gone down the road into another part of your lesson while their brains are still processing what you just did. Their nervous systems haven't reached the peak processing of the most recent task until—and possibly at the same time as—the moment that you are expecting them to attend to the next piece of the lesson. Even in the best-case scenario, information in the body travels at different rates, with some lag time between one's action and the metabolism in their system that helped them make that action. Every action we take is followed by recovery. Mental exertion, like physical exertion, is followed by a recovery period. Our bodies do this all the time. It's how we function. But, when one is learning and confronted with something new, the ebb and flow between action and recovery takes more time to resolve. It takes time to assimilate information into the body. Practice assists assimilation. Learning is about tuning that relationship so that one's attention and learning can be devoted to practicing the action that will subsequently require less recovery time as mastery improves (Ericsson, Krampe & Tesch-Römer, 1993). This is the formation of habit: to be able to execute something without having to think about it (like Bill Kirchen's guitar talent from Chapter 1). It becomes a natural part of your physiology. Think about how you guide your students (in a classroom, art studio, or outdoors). Be mindful that you're also managing these phases of execution and recovery in their nervous systems. Not only do you compete with the resting state for your students' attention, but you also compete with these processes, which also influence the readiness of your students.

Unmasking Development

It may help to picture this cycle as it unfolds across human development throughout the lifespan. A few developmental principles shape the relationship between active learning and habit formation. Here's one of the biggest: emotional development precedes cognitive development.

The Terrible Twos

Prior to the age of two, the brain is acquiring basic sensory skills for seeing, hearing, and nonverbal precursors to language (imitation, mimicry, sign language). But around the age of two, a child discovers that the world is bigger, that there's more information: more light, more sound, more people, more things going on. It isn't that the world changed overnight, it's that their brain reached a point of maturity for perceiving the complexity of the world around them. But not all of the brain makes that jump at the same time and that's why two-year-olds are classically difficult (Calkins & Williford, 2009). The prefrontal cortex isn't developed enough to process all that information, so they experience overload. While the emotional and sensory areas of the brain have developed sufficiently to absorb those kinds of information, attention processes in the frontal lobes develop *in response to* the increased amount of information that pours into the brain through their senses and emotions (Lewis, 2005).

Adolescence

Puberty brings on a similar pattern. The thalamus, a part of the brain that helps regulate basic appetites for sleep, food, and other rewards, is maturing (Cho et al., 2013). One of the tasks it practices during development is working with the insula to help generate your behavior. The insula is the part of the frontal cortex that merges the automatic self-monitoring your brain and body do to keep track of your internal states with information it gathers from the environment. It is a part of your nervous system that supports your flexibility by promoting a fluid integration of your internal (inside the body) and external (outside the body) contexts. The amygdala and hippocampus, along with other parts of the reward system, increase in volume between the ages of 7 and 22 (Goddings et al., 2014). The myelination processes of the white matter tracts that underlie mature executive functions are still working their way forward into the frontal lobes (Herting & Sowell, 2017; Mills et al., 2016; Supekar & Menon, 2012). Many of these changes are influenced by hormones. There are subtle neural differences in these processes between boys and girls that, at this time, are not known to impact executive function behaviors. This helps discount gender differences in brain development during adolescence that can account for cognitive behavior differences.

Middle school is its own universe; there's a saying among teachers that you either love it or hate it. What's the defining feature? Neurologically, the frontal lobes and the thalamus are in somewhat of a tug-of-war. What you see is a student whose behavior varies from one day, or week, to the next. One day they appear the model of young adult maturity. The next day, their behavior is so foolish that you hardly recognize them as the same student you saw the day before. Masking occurs in a big way at the middle school ages. The persistent neuromyth that students in puberty lose their capacity to learn was debunked in the Organization for Economic Cooperation and Development's (OECD) book, *Understanding the Brain: The Birth of a Learning Science*. They define adolescent brain development as a time characterized by "high horsepower and poor steering" (2007, p. 2). The neural basis of that high horsepower emanates from the shifts going on in reward neurochemistry, the dopamine system. The fluctuations of neurochemistry and hormones actually prime learning at this age. Passions run high at this stage of development. It's an *optimal* time to engage learning. I believe that people who become lifelong learners got the bug in middle school. Remember, the brain has one motivation and reward system. We typically hear about it in relationship to substance use and abuse statistics in teenagers. But, there is as high a likelihood that those same neural systems will get captured by or appropriated for a passion for learning. Just as emotions catalyze the learning process during the terrible twos, puberty is another developmental period when activity in cognitive neural systems is heightened to stretch and mature in response to emotions, hormonal changes, and increasing complexity. If a passion for learning strikes during this time, the dopamine system is going to help form habits that reinforce those interests and passions.

These are some of the physical shifts happening inside the brain and the body that influence a person's relationship with stress and challenge. Keeping this dynamic in mind as you observe how your students respond to stress, whether their responses are habit driven or more situational, can help you distinguish between positive and negative stress. Learning feels easy when it's natural—a sensible and relevant part of a real event that has social meaning and a purpose for the learner so that the learner chooses to stay, to invest themselves. Perhaps it's useful to think about the brain as a feeling organ that thinks rather than a thinking organ that feels.

Unmasking Autism

Autism is one of the most prevalent diagnoses in school-aged children today. The Centers for Disease Control (CDC) latest statistics report that 1 in 54 8-year-old children had an autism diagnosis in 2016 (Maenner et al., 2020) and 1 in 64 4-year-old children had an autism diagnosis (Shaw et al., 2020). In spite of that, our understanding of autism, particularly in children who are smart, is limited to some of the more classic features of the disorder, such as repetitive behavior, limited interests, and problems with social skills. Neuroscience has some insights to share about autism in the brain that I believe will change how you view it. Smart children (who have above average intelligence) who are on the spectrum have some underappreciated executive function strengths that point to a clear pathway for intervention (Kalbfleisch & Loughan, 2012).

A More Neutral Definition of Autism

Autism is a disorder that effects both effortful brain function and the resting state network. My colleagues and I were one of the first groups to find that the resting state does not connect and organize in people with autism like it does in the brains of neurotypical people (Washington et al., 2014). In people who have autism, the parts of the resting state, distributed all over the brain, keep to themselves instead of linking up. Furthermore, the white matter that is meant to grow into parts of the frontal lobes to support executive functions goes off course, too. The pathways reach the frontal lobes, but they arrive at differently scheduled times and at alternate locations. In the field of autism, this is described in the weak coherence hypothesis, which describes cognitive processing as detail focused on and biased toward granular levels of information rather than on the big picture (Happé & Frith, 2006). The irony is that a person with autism may perseverate on details, but they also tend to favor the inner landscape of their minds, which provides a rich internal source for their imagination, over their social context. When my research team produced this result, my first thought was, "No wonder sensory overload is a hallmark of autism." First, you have a brain whose function doesn't gel like other brains. Separate parts have to work harder on their own to support sensory, emotional, and cognitive functions. Second, because the origins of higher-level cognition begin in the back of the brain, you have a brain that tries to hold on to all of the function. In a typical child's development, those white matter fibers are programmed to grow into specific locations of the frontal lobes at distinct times (Barnea-Goraly et al., 2005; Sowell et al., 2002). In autism, the back of the brain is kind of possessive. A large share of sensory processing takes place in the back of the brain. In people with autism, these sensory processing regions try to do the job of the entire brain and hold back, delay, and alter the timing of the growth of those white matter fibers into the frontal lobes (McAlonan et al., 2009). Consequently, functions and skills develop at different times and in different locations in the brain (see Tables 4.6 and 4.7). A more neutral definition of autism spectrum disorder is this: an autistic brain is just the back of the brain trying to do the job of the whole brain. The stack is narrow and high. Picture papers piling up one on top of the other like a giant stalk. No wonder overload is so common in those with autism! In New Zealand, the Maori tribe has a word for autism, *takiwatanga*, which means "a person who experiences life in his or her own time and space" (Opai, 2017). Silberman, who wrote the book *Neurotribes: The Legacy of Autism and the Future of Neurodiversity*, says it this way: "Just because a computer is not running Windows doesn't mean that it's broken. Not all the features of atypical human operating systems are bugs" (Silberman, 2015, p. 471).

Strengths and Weaknesses in Autism

One of my graduate students and I took a closer look at the IQ discrepancy model (the numerical distance between a person's verbal and nonverbal intelligence), a model that the field of autism poses as a one of the phenotypic markers of autism (Black et al., 2009). We applied this model in a sample of children with high-functioning autism who had verbal IQ scores significantly higher than their nonverbal performance-based capacities (visual and spatial processing, nonverbal reasoning skills). We wanted to know if relationships would emerge and correlate among executive functions skills and high verbal intelligence. To look at these relationships, we used the BRIEF (Behavior Rating Inventory of Executive Function) measure because it characterizes executive function skills based on behavior observed by parents and teachers in everyday life with the children. In our review of the literature, most of the papers reported that children with autism have greater impairments in executive function than children with ADHD (Kalb-fleisch & Loughan, 2012). Furthermore, while kids with both ADHD and autism have deficits in social cognition, the deficits come from different roots. The root of social challenges in people with ADHD come from weaknesses with behavioral regulation and inhibition skills. Whereas the social challenges in people with autism come from metacognitive weaknesses with initiating and planning (Miranda et al., 2017). Among the children with high-functioning autism in our study, we found that when verbal intelligence was higher than performance intelligence by more than 1 standard deviation (15 points, the distance that clinical psychology uses to define a significant and meaningful deficit), fewer issues with executive functions associated with managing information were reported. Specifically, the behaviors of self-management—trouble inhibiting unwanted responses and shifting between tasks—were still challenged. But the skills for managing the environment (aka, every-thing else) were intact—self-starting a task, working memory capacity, monitoring a task in process, and planning and organizing a task. The take home message? In our sample of kids with autism, high verbal intelligence provided some kind of support or protection for executive function skills that apply to intellectual tasks. The opportunity pre-sented by this finding is to support these strengths educationally and leverage the students' stronger skills to support self-management in social situations. Here's what this might look like: Find a part of the curriculum that motivates the interest of your student with autism, let them delve into it and also choose other students to invite into their process (joint attention) as teammates to overlap the intellectual pro-cess (strength) with social learning (needing practice). You start with an intense focus on one interest, which is a natural feature of autism, and then entrain the student's attention to invite their teammates, to lead, teach, or guide them. You scaffold the intellectual strength into the social realm to open the possibility that what that student knows on an intellectual level (how to manage information) can transfer and lead to greater success in the social domain (transfer the strength of managing information to developing social regulation skills through sharing their expertise).

An Educator's Experiments

Unmasking Strategy 1:
Getting to the root of performance issues and executive functions.
This section is designed to help you train your eye on age-expectations for executive functions and how different disabilities and giftedness impact executive functions. Each person has their own pattern of strengths and weaknesses, which can make it hard to see exactly what's going on when a student is struggling. Look for the probable root sources of behavior in the executive functions rather than responding to the behavior itself. As a starting point, I ask two simple questions to determine if I need to tweak aspects of the environment or process in order to help student progress or if I need to circle back for more direct instruction and modeling. The answers to these two questions guide which direction I pivot in response to a struggling learner or learning moment:

1. *Do they know it but can't show it?* If so, I adjust my process or tweak something in the environment so that they can perform.
2. *Do they not know it?* If they don't know it, they need to be taught or trained.

I find that using these two questions is the most neutral way to gain insight into how to dissolve learning obstacles. Individual differences and social context can mask these two fundamental turning points in someone's learning. These questions resolve the block by giving you information so you can help students move forward without censure or self-consciousness. By answering these two questions, you help your students be poised and ready instead of overwhelmed or stuck.

A nuance underlying the use of these two questions may be that the student knows the content but lacks a certain executive function to carry out the task (planning next steps or initiating). To better understand how to get to the root of executive function challenges by identifying which skill needs support in the moment, refer to Tables 4.1 and 4.2 that present executive function skills in two prominent frameworks from research (Best & Miller, 2010; Anderson, 2002). Within each framework, I name and define the executive function skill, the age of development, how that skill is influenced by ADHD, autism, specific learning disability, and giftedness, and the skill's link to academic achievement. I hope these tables give you access to a summary of an enormous body of literature from child development, neuroscience, and education in one place that you can use to sharpen your understanding of executive functions and help you detect patterns among your students in ways you may have not been able to before. With the suggestions that come next, you can become more successful at seeing executive function behaviors for what they really are and get learning back on track.

Here are some ways to bring to light the root causes of behaviors and help students get unstuck when they fall into thought patterns that keep them from being responsive. When someone is deep in thought, out of touch with the world, and doesn't respond to the call of their name, it may be due to one of three states: perseveration, rumination, or flow (see Table 4.3). Address each one differently. For example, autism, obsessive–compulsive disorder, anxiety disorder, and other mental illnesses can cause perseveration, a repetitive unproductive focus on one thing. Use a joint attention strategy to bring students who express these conditions back into the class. For instance, use rhythm, or ask this student to help another student with a physical task. Rumination can lead to or be caused by mood imbalances and depression. Unhealthy forms of rumination include thought patterns with a persistent focus on negative aspects of oneself, such as brooding or dwelling (Beaty et al., 2019; Shapero et al., 2017). Adolescents often fall into this state of dissatisfaction with various aspects of their lives. Girls can be particularly vulnerable to the negative effects of rumination (Burwell & Shirk, 2007). Counterbalancing this, self-reflection is a positive type of rumination that involves analyzing a problem or challenge in order to devise a solution or learn from the circumstance. Positive self-reflective rumination can be good for creativity (Cohen & Ferrari, 2010). If you catch a student in a state of negative rumination, give them an analytical task that requires them to break down and devise a solution to a problem. Also, see Strategy 3

Executive Function	Skill Description	Age of Development	Affected by ADHD	Affected by Autism	Affected by Specific Learning Disability (e.g. dyslexia, dysgraphia, dyscalculia)	Influenced by Giftedness	Linked to Achievement
Attentional Control	Shift	1 3-can execute a single switch 5-can demonstrate flexibility over multiple switches	Impaired	Impaired	Can be impaired	Yes	Math, phonological awareness, letter-word identification
	Inhibit instinctive behaviors	3	Impaired	Impaired	Can be impaired	Yes	English, math, and science
	Impulse control	6 Temporarily increases between 11 and 12	Impaired	Impaired	Can be impaired	Yes	English, math, and science
	Monitor and regulate actions	9	Impaired	Impaired	Can be impaired	Yes	English, math, and science
	Switch between tasks	5-8 acquiring expertise 9-11 display expertise	Impaired	Impaired	Impaired	Yes	English, math, and science
Information Processing	Response speed	3-5	Fast but risk errors due to impulsivity Slow speed related to comorbid learning disability	Fast visual skills, editing, spotting inconsistencies	Impaired	Yes High verbal comprehension predicts achievement	Math, reading, written language
	Verbal fluency Verbal Working Memory	3-5	May observe advanced verbal skills	Enhanced in Asperger's syndrome; impaired in autism and high-functioning autism	Impaired	Yes	English
	Working Memory	Grades 5-8	Can be impaired	Can be impaired	Impaired	Yes	Math
	Processing speed	9-10, 11-12	Impaired	Impaired	Impaired	Fast or reflective	Math
	Efficiency and fluency	15	Impaired	Impaired	Impaired	Yes	Math

Cognitive Flexibility	Perseveration declines	Early and middle childhood	Hyperfocus is a constant characteristic; can be productive	Perseveration is a constant characteristic	Fine motor and perceptual deficits hinder flexibility	Rumination may have a negative influence on flexibility	None
	Switching	3–4, Capacity to switch between two things	Impaired	Impaired	Impaired	Yes	Level of flexibility in kindergarten predicts reading, math, and science achievement in second grade
		7 through Adolescence, Capacity to switch among multiple tasks	Impaired	Impaired	Impaired	Yes	Math and reading achievement
	Learn from mistakes	Middle childhood	Impaired	Impaired	Can be impaired	Yes	Attitudes toward mistakes influence achievement
Goal Setting	Generating new concepts	4 May see a regression in skill between ages 12 and 13	Impaired	Impaired	Impaired	Yes	None
	Planning and organizational Skills	7–10	Impaired	Ok if verbal skills are strong	Impaired		General levels of achievement
	Strategic behaviors and reasoning	7–11	Impaired	Ok if verbal skills are strong	Can be impaired	Yes	General levels of achievement
	Refinement of strategies and improved decision making	Throughout adolescence	Impaired	Ok if verbal skills are strong	Can be impaired	Yes	General levels of achievement
	Sequencing	9–17	Impaired	OK if visual and verbal skills are strong	Impaired	No	Reading and math in the first 3 years of primary school

TABLE 4.1: Development of executive functions

As defined by Anderson (2002), impact of ADHD, autism, specific learning disability, giftedness, and achievement (collated from Morgan et al., 2019; Kalbfleisch, 2017, 2013, 2012; McClelland et al., 2014; Komarraju & Nadler, 2013; Assouline, Nicpon & Dockery, 2012; Cragg & Chevalier, 2012; Best, Miller & Naglieri, 2011; Geary, 2011; Rose et al., 2011; Visu-Petra et al., 2011; Morrison, Ponitz & McClelland, 2010; Luciana et al., 2009; Cragg & Nation, 2009; Bull, Espy & Wiebe, 2008; Dweck, 2008; Mayes & Calhoun, 2007; St.Clair-Thomson & Gathercole, 2006; Anderson, 2002; Zimmerman & Gordon, 2001; Kaufmann, Kalbfleisch & Castellanos, 2000)

Executive Function	Skill Description	Age of Development	ADHD	Autism	Specific Learning Disability	Giftedness	Executive Function Skill Linked to Achievement
Inhibition	Ability to withhold a behavioral response. Results in an unwanted response if impaired	4, 5–8, and 12	Impaired	Impaired	Can be impaired	May be eager to respond	English, math, and science
Inhibition	Ability to withhold a response	Competence steadily increases from 6–10, and will decrease from ages 10–17	Impaired	Impaired	Can be impaired	May be eager to respond	General academic achievement Impacts reading and math—difficulty suppressing unwanted information
	Reading errors	4–8	Often impaired	A child with hyperlexia will have few errors. Reading skill can be Impaired in autism	Can be impaired	Yes	Impacts reading—difficulty suppressing unwanted information
Working Memory	Ability to maintain and manipulate information over brief periods of time without reliance on external cues or aids	6–16	Impaired	Depends on context	Impaired	Can be enhanced Often impaired in twice exceptional children	English (verbal working memory) Science and math (visual working memory) Reading

Shift	Ability to shift between mental states, rule sets, or tasks	3–4 switch between two things 7 through adolescence switch among multiple tasks	Impaired Hyperfocus is a constant characteristic; can be productive	Impaired	Impaired	Can be enhanced Often impaired in twice exceptional children	Math achievement Phonological awareness Letter/word identification

TABLE 4.2. DEVELOPMENT OF EXECUTIVE FUNCTIONS AS DEFINED BY BEST AND MILLER (2010), IMPACT OF ADHD, AUTISM, SPECIFIC LEARNING DISABILITY, GIFTEDNESS, AND ACHIEVEMENT
Collated from Kalbfleisch, 2017, 2013, 2012; Jaekel, Eryigit-Madzwamuse & Wolke, 2016; Titz & Karbach, 2014; Willoughby et al., 2012; Best, Miller & Naglieri, 2011; Best & Miller, 2010; Clark, Pritchard & Woodward, 2010; Cragg & Nation, 2008; Alloway, Gathercole & Pickering, 2006; Passolunghi & Siegel, 2001; Kaufmann, Kalbfleisch & Castellanos, 2000; Miyake et al., 2000; Nation, 1999

in this chapter for an example of how to do this. Finally, as you watch a student concentrating, they may be in either of these states or in flow. Flow is also complete concentration on one thing, but is marked by a sense of ease, pleasure, and control over a task that has a clear goal or reward (Csikszentmihalyi, 2014). This is when the hourglass strategy can be helpful, since it is also common to lose track of time during flow.

TABLE 4.3: Strategies to help students get unstuck when they fall into thought patterns that keep them from being responsive.

States of Mind that Look "Stuck"	Strategy to Disrupt or Support
Perseveration—intense focus on or repeating an action or thought after what prompted the moment is over and has been for awhile	Joint attention
Rumination—may resemble perseveration as excessive thinking or talking about something painful, causes problems with concentration, energy, and motivation	Analytical task
Flow—full and total immersion in a task or project	Hourglass

Science Behind the Strategy

EXECUTIVE FUNCTIONS ARE INHERITED. We inherit our frontal lobes, which reason and manage our executive functions, from our family's DNA. Our genes play a large role in how well we use what we know and can do and how well we manage ourselves and everything else (Kalbfleisch, 2004, 2017). In an age where science *is* discovering the genetic bases of certain kinds of individual differences, it is imperative that we remember that we are *all* individuals with differences. For example, we know that disabilities such as autism (Hill, 2004), ADHD (Davidson, Cherry & Corkum, 2016), and dyslexia (Pennington & Olson, 2005) have a heritable trace and that executive functions tend to be weaker, develop differently, or take longer to develop in these cases. This is on top of the fact that the executive functions in typical children don't develop at the same time, although boys and girls tend to develop at similar rates (Anderson, 2002). Because certain patterns of executive function are tied to various learning and developmental disabilities, becoming familiar with those developmental profiles helps with troubleshooting on behalf of those students during instruction.

WHEN STRONGER SKILLS MASK WEAKER SKILLS. Part of determining the root causes of behavior is understanding how strengths and weaknesses present themselves in special populations of learners. Strengths can mask weaker skills, making it harder to see the root of the problem (Kalbfleisch, 2012, 2013 Kalbfleisch & Loughan, 2012). Children referred to as twice exceptional have strong capacities and talents (intellectual, artistic, athletic) and disabilities such as attention and learning disorders, psychiatric conditions, or physical conditions that effect their cognitive processing. Hence, exceptionalities on both ends of the ability curve (Kalbfleisch, 2012, 2013). Twice exceptional children with attention disorders may fail miserably at keeping their thoughts to themselves (Walcott & Landau, 2004) but have strong divergent, associational, and conceptual thinking skills (Kaufmann, Kalbfleisch, & Castellanos, 2000). Children with dyslexia lose time and parts of the lesson because their language processing computes on a different scale, but they may sail at visual problem solving and have a knack for building things and adapting existing resources to suit new purposes (Kalbfleisch, 2012). This can be difficult because different executive functions can even mask each other. For example, kids with autism and kids with ADHD can both appear distracted. But what distracts them is different. Kids with attention disorders have brains that produce lower levels of dopamine, the chemical of reward and motivation that helps one focus. Thus, kids with attention disorders don't really have a deficit. Instead, they are distracted by everything at once. Their brains lack the *filter* to naturally ignore distraction. On the other hand, kids with autism tend to be more interested in their minds, imaginations, and internal states (Kalbfleisch & Loughan, 2012). On the surface, we see a distracted child but don't readily see the root cause. You might quiet the room for the child with ADHD, but draw out and engage the child on the autism spectrum in thoughtful conversation. These responses are opposites. Table 4.3 provides a quick reference for how to disrupt negative mind and mood states.

In another example, kids with inattentive-type ADHD tend to have stronger self-management skills than productivity. So, they're good at managing themselves, but not so great at managing everything else. They're composed, agreeable, and appropriate. Because of this, they may not readily get help with their weaknesses, which tend to be with working memory and managing the demands of academic tasks whose directions have more than two steps (Davidson, Cherry, & Corkum, 2016). Kids with this kind of attention deficit easily tip over into hyperfocus, another version of flow (Kaufman, Kalbfleisch, & Castellanos, 2000).

Unmasking Strategy 2:
Develop a learning contract with your students that will guide how you and they will respond to mistakes during learning.

Everyone makes mistakes. Some kids let them roll off of their backs, others take them too much to heart, and sometimes the ones who should learn their lesson, don't. Errors are a natural part of practice and learning. The goal for this strategy is to create a healthy prospective conversation about mistakes and errors that includes understanding where they come from in the brain. I liken it to the do-over, and everybody needs one now and then. After having a conversation as a class about how the brain detects mistakes (the Science Behind the Strategy for Strategy 2 explains this), co-construct a learning contract that defines how you and your students will respond when mistakes happen. Learning contracts are a popular strategy to support diverse learning needs during differentiated instruction (Duncan, 2013; Lemieux, 2001; Tomlinson, 1995). In this case, addressing affect is the main goal. A teacher's position during differentiation is to facilitate and coach. Giving constructive feedback imparts a feeling that you have your students' backs. Whereas bald criticism can embed shame, blame, and embarrassment. Emotions that arise from criticism create cascades of adrenaline in the brain and body that can obstruct learning for several minutes or hours after it happens. This is one of those times when someone may experience low registration caused by stress. When students can understand that errors and mistakes happen naturally during learning and that the brain has a setup for detecting mistakes and using them to help us learn, the discussion elevates beyond shame, blame, and self-consciousness. The contract might read something like this: "Mistakes are a natural part of the learning process and everyone makes them from time to time. When that happens, our class agrees that we will support each other when a mistake happens, use constructive feedback when correcting a person to help them be successful on the next try, and ask questions when there is a misunderstanding. We agree that we will not blame, make fun of, or personally criticize someone who makes a mistake." Everyone will take ownership because they had a say in the formation of the contract. By establishing a healthy way to approach errors, you will build resilience in your students and keep anxiety to a minimum during tough learning moments. This is a lesson they will keep for life.

Science Behind the Strategy

ERRORS IN THE BRAIN. Let's talk about errors from the brain's point of view. Errors are like hiccups in the learning process as one practices toward mastery. Mistakes are a natural part of the learning curve. A person's relationship with making errors and mistakes matters. Dweck's research on fixed versus growth mindsets has shown us that students who believe that their levels of intelligence can be changed with learning experience higher levels of achievement (Dweck, 2008, 2014; Blackwell et al., 2007). The difference between mindsets has to do with how students internalize

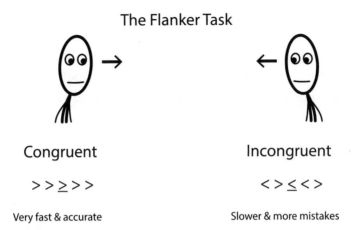

The Flanker Task

Congruent

> > ≥ > >

Very fast & accurate

Incongruent

< > ≤ < >

Slower & more mistakes

FIGURE 4.1: Looking at Errors in the Brain

their experiences with learning and whether their efforts amount to success, or the difference between developing learned helplessness versus learning from mistakes. The exciting thing is that Dweck proved this difference in studies with middle schoolers in math and science, smashing the myth that puberty keeps adolescents from learning. Students' beliefs about themselves were the key influence driving the relationship between how they viewed their ability level and how well they achieved.

In some cases, errors can be detected in the brain up to a half a minute before you actually make them. An imaging experiment designed to look at how well people control their attention showed us this fascinating feature of learning. The experiment required people to perform the flanker task, one of the most well-studied tasks in psychology and neuroscience (Verbruggen et al., 2006; Eriksen & Eriksen, 1974). It's a visual game based on pictures of rows of arrows (see Figure 4.1). In the congruent condition, all of the arrows point in the same direction. There are five arrows in each presentation, and the person is asked to focus on the middle arrow and to press a button that corresponds with the direction of the middle arrow. When all five arrows are pointing in the same direction, a person's response time is very fast and very accurate. As soon as you change the directions of some of those arrows, a person's performance slows down and their accuracy decreases. It isn't that their brain can't do the task; it's that the brain's braking system is getting involved, taking just a bit longer to recognize and press a button, because when the arrows in the line point in different directions, deciphering takes longer.

One of the ways neuroscientists study mistakes in the brain involves looking at how fast someone can control their attention during a visual game called the flanker task (Eriksen & Eriksen, 1974). Subjects look at the row of arrows and are instructed to indicate which direction the middle arrow is pointing (right or left) as fast as they can. Imagine doing this with about 100 pictures in a row made up of congruent and incongruent strings of arrows!

An international research team led by Tom Eichele (2008) used the flanker task in an fMRI experiment and then analyzed the instances when the subjects made a mistake. Through a series of computations, they were able to trace back to the point where the brain was toggling between responses. Imagine the brain saying to itself, "Which direction is the arrow pointing, and how fast can I press the button to give a response?", well before the person actually responds (Eichele et al., 2008). In some cases, researchers were able to detect the point of error 24 to 30 seconds before the subject actually made it. Now, you may be thinking, how could you possibly know what a student is going to do a half a minute before they actually do it? You can't, but the teachable moment from this finding is that the brain is always slightly ahead of what the body does. Even if the BOLD response is slower! Analysis of the data Eichele's team collected showed that the resting state was intruding on effortful processing during the task, which was to press a button to indicate the direction of the middle arrow. Let me explain further with an analogy. Imagine the resting state system and the attention system in the brain, which is required to perform the flanker task, as a baseball game with all the bases loaded. The player (attention) on first base is queued up and ready to run (focused on the arrows), while teammates on second and third bases are distracted (resting state activity). Attention may eventually get to home, but in fits and starts, while the players ahead of it either cross home plate or strike out. While the person was playing the flanker task, which moves at a very fast clip, the brain was anticipating the different directions of the arrows in the game, but the resting state was also trying to do its job of monitoring and balancing the overall system. When accuracy isn't perfect, it's because the brain is practicing at coordinating these systems. When accuracy is perfect, that means the skill is well learned. This is another example from neuroscience showing us how the brain orchestrates learning.

I like to suggest the idea that your brain has your back. After learning about the 24-second lead the brain has, you may be wondering whether you indeed have free will and a sense of choice. You do. It isn't that your brain is determining what you will do before you decide to do it. Rather, your senses and perception, like the resting state, prepare you to take action by grabbing on to some bits of the problem before others. The brain does its best to coordinate input from your senses, information from your environment and from your emotions, to position you for success, and practice improves the odds. That's the power behind the insight that early childhood attention training, using computer games that operate like the flanker task, supports the development of emotional control and lays the foundation for the development of other executive functions (Rueda, Posner & Rothbart, 2005). Remember, emotional development happens first, and cognitive skills develop in response.

The value of educating your students about the function of errors serves two purposes on a behavioral level. First, you are teaching the brains of your students the behavioral policies of learning—giving them feedback so that they can respond and improve their efficiency with practice. As Tables 4.1 and 4.2 on the development of executive functions illustrate, children don't acquire skills and knowledge all at once, and individual differences make the picture even more complex. Second, you are coaching your students to regard mistakes as tools and information rather than emotional downfalls. What about feedback and constructive criticism? Every human is sensitive to being criticized in front of other people. Shame causes a cascade of activity in the brain in the neural systems we've been discussing that relate to self-reference and internal states (Zhu et al., 2019). Fear of embarrassment and humiliation hijack the working memory systems in the brain (Kreifelts et al., 2014). Often, the levels of self-consciousness associated with puberty and adolescence mean that you may be competing with the fact their minds are already primed to be more sensitive and perceptive in this way (Dahl & Gunnar, 2009). It's the fine line between a person perceiving that you are laughing at them, when, in fact, you are laughing with them. A moment of embarrassment, shame, or self-consciousness can singlehandedly derail learning. Working memory will encode everything negative about that timepoint and cause your student to miss the moment or the lesson at hand. Like a nonstick coating, raised levels of threat in a learning moment will deflect what you are trying to impart.

Unmasking Strategy 3:
Unmask threat, stress, and anxiety with analogy, metaphor, and divergent thinking.

This strategy can help you disrupt stress and get students' thinking on track. Just as you can teach the class about the importance of mistakes during learning, it's also important to talk about the neurobiology of stress, good and bad, and how it relates to feeling challenged. To introduce the conversation to your students about the relationship between stress and challenge, use the guidance from the earlier sections of this chapter on stress, low registration, and BOLD response. Then, find a picture of a maze, such as the one in Figure 4.2.

Pose the open question, "How is fear like a maze?" Let the discussion unfold. So many different responses can come from that question. Some students I have worked with on this have responded with, "You can't see to the end," "You try a lot of different ideas and nothing works," or "It takes a lot of tries to get to the end." Some students respond to the challenge positively with, "If you have to keep trying, you get a lot of turns." The first response of each student is going to teach you about their point of view. Are they ruminating, self-reflecting, motivated, or defeated? Remember that positive self-reflective rumination can be good for creativity (Verhaegan, Joorman & Aikman, 2014). Document their responses so that after the discussion, you will have information that will help you find ways to relieve stress and anxiety because you will begin to understand more about how each of them tends to idle—is their glass half empty or half full? Afterward, ask your students directly how you can support them. Throughout this exercise they will also be listening and

FIGURE 4.2: Use a maze as a visual prompt for a discussion about the relationship between stress and challenge.

learning how to help each other. Refer back to the experimental strategies in Chapter 3 to help your students tip their dispositions from self-centered to team-centered.

Science Behind the Strategy

HIGHER-LEVEL THINKING CAN DISRUPT STRESS. This is another strategy based on mindfulness and using challenging or stimulating intellectual tasks to override a stress response. The goal with this strategy is to use higher-level thinking to influence, disrupt, and extract a student from an anxious state. Our frontal lobes influence how and how well we manage emotion (Goldsmith & Davidson, 2004). One of the ways they do that is to help the brain match the context of the external environment. As we've discussed, in children, the frontal lobes are in constant development and do not reach full maturity until well beyond the school-aged years. The hippocampus also plays a role in processing context; it helps us navigate and understand where we are in a physical space (Davidson et al., 2000). Remember that chronic stress damages and shrinks hippocampal neurons, which blunts or dulls a person's response to stress, and can impair memory over time. Disrupting behaviors and states of mind happening during negative stress result in powerful moments of intervention when challenges become overwhelming.

A critical insight about rumination is that it can be used constructively. Rumination can be task-focused (concentrating on the task at hand or something related to it), state-focused (mood-related), or completely unrelated to the context (Ciarocco et al., 2010). If a student is ruminating because of a mistake, it can be positive if they are focused on correcting their error and getting back on track. Motivation has a lot to do with the quality of rumination. Having students use their eyes to focus on solving a visual puzzle can swing their motivation so that their energies shift to problem solving. The maze task suggested here adds another dimension by using analogy to draw out feelings from the students. This approach is reminiscent of the research on phantom-limb syndrome that proved that we can use our eyes to disrupt pain and anxiety (Ramachandran & Rogers-Ramachandran, 2000; Ramachandran & Hirstein, 1998).

Unmasking Strategy 4:
Add "for now" to the end of a student's description
of their struggle to interrupt the flow of anxiety and
bring their attention back to the present.

I developed this strategy working with adults on retreat. Just as I use Almonds and Cherries with populations of all ages, in schools and in my practice, I also use the phrase or mantra "For Now" to help people learn to curb overwhelm and sensory overload. On a hike during a retreat I hosted in the winter of 2015, one of my participants sat down for a break in the middle of a beautiful field and began to exclaim her problems in one of those sentences that seems to stretch on forever without taking a breath. I was sitting across from her and it occurred to me to say to her in response, "Put these two words at the end of your sentence: *for now.* Whenever you are talking about your stress, distress, or discomfort finish the sentence with 'for now.'" Just as a period punctuates the end of a sentence, these two words keep the feelings in the present. "For now" suggests there will be an end to whatever is bothering us. What feels like it could last forever, won't. This has become a simple way to coach people to halt anxiety and stress in their mind and body. When we are in a state of worry or anxiety, it's common for our self-talk and inner speech to run on like a stock market ticker tape. The next time you are in a situation like this, when a student or colleague is overtaken with temporary panic, anxiety, or stress, talk with them about what's on their mind. At the end of their statement about what's wrong, ask them to add the words "for now." Using "for now" to punctuate our nervous thoughts signals the body that these thoughts do not have to be overwhelming. Whatever is wrong, it's temporary. For example, if a student tells you that they are worried about how they will do on the test because they didn't prepare, add "for now" to the end of the sentence. Or, they tell you that they are arguing with a friend or broke up with someone and so they can't concentrate or finish their big project—"for now." Full stop. Period. Get them to see their troubles and anxieties as situational—for now—and encourage them to stop that train of thought, come back to the present moment, and move on to something else. It's no wonder we call our brain a "nervous" system.

Science Behind the Strategy

USING MINDFULNESS TECHNIQUES TO REDUCE STRESS. John Kabat-Zinn, the creator of Mindfulness Based Stress Reduction (MSBR), defines the practice as "paying attention in a particular way: on purpose, in the present moment, and nonjudgmentally" (Kabat-Zinn, 2009). With this definition in mind, the power in the For Now technique is that it brings a person's attention to the moment, cutting off the ticker-tape talking inside their head, and encourages them to slow down and consider what's happening from a different perspective. Language influences the perception of emotion (Lindquist et al., 2006). Now is the present. Putting a full stop period on the end of the sentence punctuates it, creating the pause for a breath that can halt the sense of overwhelm. There is a burgeoning agenda in neuroscience to apply these kinds of practices and techniques to education because studies have shown they influence brain plasticity, the immune system, and emotion processing (Tang, Hölzel & Posner, 2015; Tang et al., 2012; Lutz et al., 2008; Davidson et al., 2003; Davidson et al., 2000). The meta-analysis of SEL programs discussed in Chapter 3 (Durlak et al., 2011) are a part of this effort to bring empathy and better mental health to the learning process in schools.

Unmasking Strategy 5:
Identify the lonely, disconnected, or bullied.

This strategy is not mine, but when I read it, I felt compelled to include it because it touches on an important aspect of masking—finding students who are at-risk for bullying and loneliness. Glennon Doyle, the author of *Love Warrior*, gives an account on her blog, "Momastery," about one teacher's strategy for social justice in her classroom. It's brilliant and can be applied to any classroom and any age with some thought on how to fit it to your practice. It goes like this. Once a week, ask students to jot the following thoughts down on a piece of paper:

1. Write down the names of two to four people you would like to sit with or do group work with when you start the next lesson or project.
2. Name one student who has displayed great citizenship or leadership.

Then, analyze the responses to determine the following:

1. Who is not getting requested by anyone else?
2. Who doesn't even know who to request?
3. Who never gets noticed enough to be nominated?
4. Who had a million friends last week and none this week?

This exercise allows you to pinpoint potential bullies and those being bullied, as well as those who may need some assertive intervention to learn how to connect and make friends. When Glennon asked her son's teacher how long she had been doing this, she replied, "Ever since Columbine."

Science Behind the Strategy

ADVERSE CHILDHOOD EVENTS (ACES). A modern source of trauma comes from adverse childhood events (ACE). ACES are experienced by more children than we realize: today, 28% experience physical abuse, 27% experience substance abuse, 13% experience domestic violence, and 20% experience sexual abuse. Compared to their unaffected counterparts, these children are twice as likely to develop heart disease, three times as likely to suffer from depression, and are at risk for a life expectancy reduction of up to 20 years (Edwards, 2018). Children in these circumstances are likely not only to experience these traumas but also to inherit them from multiple generations of their family who have lived with the same influences. The field of epigenetics shows us that behavior and temperament can be inherited just as physical conditions are passed on in families (Heim & Binder, 2012; Matthews & Phillips, 2012). Thus, the presenting behaviors may be compounded by a child's family history, and not just the immediate setting or situation (Walters et al., 2011). Receiving mistreatment at home or in school can result in the same kind of trauma. The brain doesn't distinguish the source. The hypothalamic–pituitary–adrenal (HPA) axis is the system in the brain and body that regulates stress. This system is heavily regulated by cortisol (and adrenalin), and when someone is under stress, the HPA runs at a high level, dumping stress hormones into the body and brain. A recent child development study (Roubinov et al., 2020) followed a group of children as they transitioned into kindergarten, through fall and into spring, and identified three distinct profiles of stress responses: (1) kids with heightened HPA-axis activity, whom they refer to as "responders"; (2) kids with appropriate and adapting levels of stress, whom they refer to as "active copers/mobilizers"; and (3) kids with heightened levels of baseline activity, whom they refer to as "anticipatory/arousal responders." As they monitored the students from fall to spring, these patterns remained stable, leading the researchers to conclude that this is a reliable marker for identifying children this young who may be at risk of developing a stressful coping response.

Neuromyth Checkpoint: Assumptions to Question

Assumption 1:
Take your students at face value.

You know the old adage, don't judge a book by its cover. That is the essential message in this chapter. Learning is made up of so much more than just remembering—there are several layers of the onion to peel back before you get to the heart of why a student struggles. The learning sciences are showing us just how many more layers there are to understand. I hope that this book will help you sharpen your diagnostic capacity during instruction and that it will leave your mind excited and energized with new understanding and fresh motivation to try some new things.

Assumption 2:
Low registration means a person doesn't feel anything in the moment.

A person with low registration *does* experience their world in real time. It may take longer for some to express the cumulative emotional impact of something that has happened. A student who has slow processing speed may anticipate something with great excitement, but when the moment comes, they may not be ready to participate. You may wonder why they won't engage after being excited for so long. If their anticipation has been highly arousing and emotional, this, itself, may delay their capacity to engage intellectually. The intention behind using my techniques (almonds and cherries, for now) and critical thinking to disrupt stress is to try to bring those who are processing a lot of emotion and anxiety into the present moment more quickly.

Assumption 3:

Learning amounts to remembering something or demonstrating a skill.
On the contrary, the learning process is not linear. Rote memorization and rehearsal are only small pieces of what memory does for us. We tend to consider learning synonymous with memory, but it's much more than that—learning is also processing sensations and feelings and developing executive functions, learned behaviors, habits, mindsets, our reflexes, and emotional responses. In particular, we have struggled with ways to identify and teach executive functions that lead to meaningful transfer. Learning is about gaining knowledge and skills, but executive functions are the gatekeepers for how and how well you use what you know and what you can do.

Assumption 4:

You can teach a student to master their executive functions within a year.
Because executive functions are constantly developing throughout the school years and don't fully mature until a person is in their mid-20s, you may not get to see the fruits of your efforts to teach and coach executive function skills in your students. Even when one skill is focused on at a developmentally appropriate time, the results will likely not be immediate.

TAKEAWAYS FOR SMALL BUT POWERFUL CHANGES IN PRACTICE

➤ Context matters. Is it that your student knows it but is having trouble showing it? If so, change the context. If they don't know it, they need to be taught and trained.

➤ Stress, low registration, and the BOLD response all influence the speed of neural processing and may slow a person's response to what's being asked of them and what's going on around them.

➤ Examine the executive functions. Look beyond what you think you see to what's really happening. Look for the probable causes of behavior in the executive functions, as the root source, rather than responding to the behavior itself.

➤ Language has the power to help regulate emotion through expression

and the ability to shape higher-level thinking. Employ language techniques to help students re-direct and manage their emotions during
learning.

➤ Use their eyes to help their brains. Use high-level visuals such as mazes
and puzzles to disrupt negative thinking with analytical challenges.

Conclusion

Adjusting to Schooling and Learning in Pandemic Times

As I write this, we are continuing to navigate the COVID-19 pandemic. Schooling changed acutely and dramatically in the spring of 2020. By the time you read this, there may have been more iterations and adjustments to how we *do* school. Are we in person or online? Learning through blended hybrid instruction or remotely? Homeschool takes on new meaning. I have begun to conceptualize it as home/school in cases where parents are juggling jobs, the care of their children, internet access, and the requirements and demands of school routines for their children. Whatever the circumstance you find yourself in at this moment, I want to encourage you to remember two things.

First, the neurological insights and misunderstandings presented in each chapter apply to everyone. The four tenets that are highlighted, each in its own chapter—flexibility, readiness, connection, and masking—are about fundamental ways our brains and bodies are wired to learn that are underserved by current conceptions and teaching practices. The basic physical organization of our nervous system is an *endogenous heuristic*, which translates to mean a map or a blueprint (heuristic) inside of our bodies (endogenous; Kalbfleisch, 2008). Your brain is as unique as your fingerprint. No two are the same. Though we share in common a basic neurology, there are differences in brain connectivity that make each of us unique. We each have our own playbook of sorts. We inherit our frontal lobes, which reason and manage executive functions, from our family via DNA. But the areas of the brain that support language, emotion, and memory are more open to influence from the environment. How you use what you learn may be governed by what you inherit from your family, but your capacity to learn from experience, to acquire knowledge, and to pursue your interests is unlimited (Kalbfleisch, 2004). Just as the architecture in Chaco Canyon is a physical foundation and connection to the abstract concepts of astronomy and physics that extend beyond the ruins, so the physical brain gives rise to the cognition and behavior we see that originates within and emerges from each of us.

Second, the strategies that are recommended for the classroom can also be adapted for online and informal learning settings. For instance, online platforms are already engineered to facilitate group work within classes. Strategies like the Reverse Quiz can also be adapted to the online environment. Spaced learning is a natural fit for the gaps of time between class sessions. Instead of worrying about efficiency, anticipate these gaps and use them to benefit student learning. Your students may not be able to be in a physical enriched classroom environment of your making. But I hope that all of the ways I've talked about using distraction to serve learning will be ways you can optimize your reach and influence your students who may be learning online from homes that are full of distractions. Informal learning may lead the way as art teachers, yogis, naturalists, athletes, and scientists become inspired to take learning outside, where it may be safest to gather and re-establish the sense of team and connection we all need.

One of my favorite quotes comes from U.S. Poet Laureate, Joy Harjo. It captures my sentiment on how important it is, in this moment of education, to reinvigorate the mental health of teachers and students alike and to make sure that our brains get to practice being flexible, ready, connected, and understood. In an interview with The Legacy Project: Growth Hack Your Life (2015), when asked how she copes with doubt Harjo responded, "I have learned to step back, take the time, if possible, to process what is coming at me. I don't want to be a person who reacts. Rather, someone who acts gracefully and calmly from within, no matter what comes at me." Cultivating brains that are flexible, ready, connected, and understood by others and themselves will prepare students to appreciate and cultivate a balance between their autonomy and relatedness, their "roots and wings" (Rothbaum & Trommsdorff, 2007, p. 464). The essence of an adaptive brain manifests as someone who can respond appropriately no matter what they are faced with, who experiences and maintains that state of play and readiness even when their surroundings might be chaotic, who is buoyed by a social safety net, and who can advocate for themselves when the context doesn't fit. Learning to meet the goals and standards set in school to achieve and advance is a reality and a defining feature of public and higher education, but what it means to be educated goes beyond that. Education isn't just knowing facts and imparting skills in certain contexts only. Ultimately, education helps us develop a capacity for discernment and judgement that will serve us throughout life. At its best, education positions a person to be able to choose the relationships, experiences, vocations, and avocations that bring out their best.

Brian Herbert, a coauthor of the *Dune* series, coined this phrase in the book *Dune: House Harkonnen*: "The capacity to learn is a gift. The ability to learn is a skill. The willingness to learn is a choice" (Herbert & Anderson, 2003, p. 532). The optimal classroom keeps all three of those elements in balance. The concept of the enriched environment in neuroscience is a powerful one for education. Neuroscientist Marian Diamond performed the first studies that looked at what we call an enriched environment and successfully captured the influence that the environment exerts on learning (Diamond, 1966a). She performed her studies by observing rat behavior. She noticed that rats who were caged alone behaved differently than those that were given periods of interaction. The first time I saw a picture of the complex, enriched environment, it reminded me of a playground or a preschool classroom; the environment had tunnels, rolling balls, open spaces, and places for the animals to run, forage, chase, hide and explore. Diamond learned that putting animals in environments like this resulted in the development of thicker cortices and more neurons in the hippocampal area, the brain region that kickstarts the memory process (Diamond et al., 1966b). What we've been able to learn from those experiments is how exquisitely sensitive the brain is to experience. Knowing that all of your students bring a capacity to learn (the gift), that you are teaching them skills necessary for classroom success and for life (the ability), and that, on some level, they choose to give attention to you and their learning (the choice). You want them to make that choice every day. And you have the chance to reaffirm that choice within yourself. It's important to know that the brain is going to develop in spite of what's going on and, we hope, because of what's going on and that it has its own clock, its own timing mechanisms for which pathways develop when and with what quality. A teacher is like a gardener. The thing to do is see through to the root of a problem or a behavior, provide or facilitate an appropriate remedy to address the actual problem, and clear the path.

A good conversation about differentiation addresses knowledge, process, and product. For your knowledge, maintain the insight that there are processes already present in your brain, your mind, and your body that are there to protect you and keep you well. Csikszentmihalyi (1990) says it well when he exclaims, "The best moments in our lives are not the passive, receptive, relaxing times . . . The best moments usually occur if a person's body or mind is stretched to its limits in a voluntary effort to accomplish something difficult and worthwhile" (1990, p. 3). For your process, what do you do with that self-knowledge and, as a teacher, with the knowledge you glean about your students?

As for thinking about product, I hope two things happen. First, that you feel some personal relief that you can work on behalf of all your students and be practiced enough that you won't feel daunted when a really challenging class full of students, who don't quite fit well with each other or with your own teaching style, comes your way. By applying the principles—to support the development of skills (flexibility, readiness, connection, and unmasking)—and strategies in this book, you can establish an enriched learning environment.

Second, I hope this book helps you shift and deepen how you view your role as a teacher. It's important to know that dendrites in our brain's gray matter are exquisitely tuned to perceive moments and sensations. They are tuned to the environment and—like open baseball mitts, poised to field a line drive and catch a fly ball—are receptive and responsive to the information they receive. Neurons are incredibly sensitive. So sensitive, we know, that if somebody endures a period of extended boredom, dendrites can shrink and neurons detach from one another, a bit like broken weave on a basket coming apart. We also know that chronic stress and forms of depression do the same thing to dendrites, causing them to atrophy and withdraw from their matrices. Neurons have their own readiness state, attained by a combination of their chemistry and information from the environment. Once neurons become active, whether to embed a new skill into muscle memory or encode new information into the brain, their physical shape, literally, will change in response to that learning. There are changes occurring beyond the learning and behavior that you see. The enriched environment experiments are at the root of that knowledge, showing us how the nurture process influences the quality of brain development. Those dendritic changes are the physical evidence of learning. We can't see this change with the naked eye, but you can see the changes in behavior and knowledge in your students during learning, which are the outward signs of these changes.

There is a great deal of individual variation in the brain's architecture. For instance, a common benchmark in child neurology claims that before a child is 7 years of age, the nervous system has the capacity to exhibit wide and wild behavioral differences. "Normal" connotes a broad range. This is why it is recommended that psychiatric disorders not be diagnosed until after age 7. The brain is also plastic and resilient. Hemispherectomy surgery is sometimes performed in early childhood to remove the part of a child's brain that is causing intractable seizures (Battro, 2003). In a hemispherectomy, one hemisphere, or half of the brain, is surgically removed. The intelligence of children who have undergone this procedure is untouched. Following recovery, the only outward indication of this surgery tends to be that one side of the body is a little more stiff than the other, due to the loss of motor pathways from the hemispherectomy, which support function on the opposite side of the body. This evidence of neuroplasticity has staggering implications for education and how teachers regard students and their potential limitations. There is no place in the classroom for an assumption that someone can't learn. Everyone's endogenous heuristic is slightly different, but all contain the capacity for learning. There are essential but not-so-basic skill sets that we are all born with that begin to function soon after birth: the skills to detect agency, who or what initiates or influences an action (Spelke & Kinzler, 2007; Saxe, Tenenbaum & Carey, 2005), imbalances of power (Gülgöz and Gelman, 2017), auditory inconsistencies in speech and language differences

(Kuhl, 2010), and deception (Wimmer & Perner, 1983). In these ways, our minds are, from the outset, smarter than we realize. In neuroimaging studies, there are significant computational resources dedicated to analyzing signal that comes from the human brain during fMRI. This process involves fitting and stacking all of the images acquired from people who participated in the study into the same compartment in order to find the signals that are common across each of those brains. It takes a lot of computational power to do that because of the fingerprint-like variation from one brain to another. Neuroscientists aren't the only ones who have to work hard to "fit" different brains into a common space. Teachers contend with that same challenge! Knowledge and insight happen when learning from the inside out meets and matches learning from the outside in. You are in a position to make sure that the meeting is a fruitful one and that students who might otherwise worry they are doomed to fail will be groomed to sail.

References

Abler, B., Walter, H., Erk, S., Kammerer, H., & Spitzer, M. (2006). Prediction error as a linear function of reward probability is coded in human nucleus accumbens. *Neuroimage, 31*(2), 790–795.

Adler, M. (1982). A Revolution in Education. *American Educator, 6*(4), 20–24.

Agnati, L. F., Guidolin, D., Battistin, L., Pagnoni, G., & Fuxe, K. (2013). The neurobiology of imagination: possible role of interaction-dominant dynamics and default mode network. *Frontiers in Psychology, 4*, 296.

Alloway, T. P., Gathercole, S. E., & Pickering, S. J. (2006). Verbal and visuospatial short-term and working memory in children: Are they separable? *Child Development, 77*(6), 1698–1716.

Amabile, T. M. (2018). *Creativity in context: Update to the social psychology of creativity*. Routledge.

Amabile, T. M., Barsade, S. G., Mueller, J. S., & Staw, B. M. (2005). Affect and creativity at work. *Administrative Science Quarterly, 50*(3), 367–403.

Anderson, P. (2002). Assessment and development of executive function (EF) during childhood. *Child Neuropsychology, 8*(2), 71–82.

Aronson, E., & Bridgeman, D. (1979). Jigsaw groups and the desegregated classroom: In pursuit of common goals. *Personality and Social Psychology Bulletin, 5*(4), 438–446.

Assouline, S. G., Nicpon, M. F., & Dockery, L. (2012). Predicting the academic achievement of gifted students with autism spectrum disorder. *Journal of Autism and Developmental Disorders, 42*(9), 1781–1789.

Atchley, R. A., Strayer, D. L., & Atchley, P. (2012). Creativity in the wild: Improving creative reasoning through immersion in natural settings. *PloS One, 7*(12), e51474.

Awh, E., Barton, B., & Vogel, E. K. (2007). Visual working memory represents a fixed number of items regardless of complexity. *Psychological Science, 18*(7), 622–628.

Babiloni, F., & Astolfi, L. (2014). Social neuroscience and hyperscanning techniques: past, present and future. *Neuroscience & Biobehavioral Reviews, 44*, 76–93.Baddeley, A. (1994). The magical number seven: Still magic after all these years? *Psychological Review, 101*, 353–356.

Baird, B., Smallwood, J., Mrazek, M. D., Kam, J. W., Franklin, M. S., & Schooler, J. W. (2012). Inspired by distraction: Mind wandering facilitates creative incubation. *Psychological Science, 23*, 1117–1122.

Bal, P. M., & Veltkamp, M. (2013). How does fiction reading influence empathy? An experimental investigation on the role of emotional transportation. *PloS One, 8*(1), e55341.

Bandura, A. (1982). Self-efficacy mechanism in human agency. *American Psychologist, 37*(2), 122.

Barnea-Goraly, N., Menon, V., Eckert, M., Tamm, L., Bammer, R., Karchemskiy, A., Dant, C. C., & Reiss, A. L. (2005). White matter development during childhood and adolescence: a cross-sectional diffusion tensor imaging study. *Cerebral Cortex, 15*(12), 1848–1854.

Bayliss, D. M., Jarrold, C., Gunn, D. M., & Baddeley, A. D. (2003). The complexities of complex span: Explaining individual differences in working memory in children and adults. *Journal of Experimental Psychology: General, 132*(1), 71.

Beaty, R. E., Benedek, M., Silvia, P. J., & Schacter, D. L. (2016). Creative cognition and brain network dynamics. *Trends in Cognitive Sciences, 20*(2), 87–95.

Beaty, R. E., Benedek, M., Wilkins, R. W., Jauk, E., Fink, A., Silvia, P. J., Hodges, D. A., Koschutnig, K., & Neubauer, A. C. (2014). Creativity and the default network: A functional connectivity analysis of the creative brain at rest. *Neuropsychologia, 64*, 92–98.

Beaty, R. E., Seli, P., & Schacter, D. L. (2019). Thinking about the past and future in daily life: an experience sampling study of individual differences in mental time travel. *Psychological Research, 83*(4), 805–816.

Berrett, D. (2012, February 19). How 'flipping' the classroom can improve the traditional lecture. *The Chronicle of Higher Education, 2*(19), 1–3.

Best, J. R., & Miller, P. H. (2010). A developmental perspective on executive function. *Child Development, 81*(6), 1641–1660.

Best, J. R., Miller, P. H., & Naglieri, J. A. (2011). Relations between executive function and academic achievement from ages 5 to 17 in a large, representative national sample. *Learning and Individual Differences, 21*(4), 327–336.

Bevilacqua, D., Davidesco, I., Wan, L., Chaloner, K., Rowland, J., Ding, M., Poeppel, D. & Dikker, S. (2019). Brain-to-brain synchrony and learning outcomes vary by student–teacher dynamics: Evidence from a real-world classroom electroencephalography study. *Journal of Cognitive Neuroscience, 31*(3), 401–411.

Bhattacharya, J. (2017). Cognitive neuroscience: Synchronizing brains in the classroom. *Current   Biology, 27*(9), R346–R348.

Bialystok, E., & DePape, A. M. (2009). Musical expertise, bilingualism, and executive functioning. *Journal of Experimental Psychology: Human Perception and Performance, 35*(2), 565.

Blaas, S. (2014). The relationship between social-emotional difficulties and underachievement of gifted students. *Journal of Psychologists and Counsellors in Schools, 24*(2), 243–255.

Black, D. O., Wallace, G. L., Sokoloff, J. L., & Kenworthy, L. (2009). Brief report: IQ split predicts social symptoms and communication abilities in high-functioning children with autism spectrum disorders. *Journal of Autism and Developmental Disorders, 39*(11), 1613–1619.

Blackwell, L. S., Trzesniewski, K. H., & Dweck, C. S. (2007). Implicit theories of intelligence predict achievement across an adolescent transition: A longitudinal study and an intervention. *Child Development, 78*(1), 246–263.

Blakemore, S. J., & Choudhury, S. (2006). Development of the adolescent brain: implications for executive function and social cognition. *Journal of Child Psychology and Psychiatry, 47*(3–4), 296–312.

Bloom, D. (April 26, 2016). Instead of detention, these students get meditation. *CNN.* Retrieved from https://www.cnn.com/2016/11/04/health/meditation-in-schools-baltimore/index.html

Bond, N. (2007). Questioning strategies that minimize classroom management problems. *Kappa Delta Pi Record, 44*(1), 18–21.

Boyle, N. (2020). *Classroom Reading to Engage the Heart and Mind: 200+ Picture Books to Start SEL Conversations.* W. W. Norton & Company.

Bransford, J. D., Sherwood, R. D., Hasselbring, T. S., Kinzer, C. K., & Williams, S. M. (1990). Anchored instruction: Why we need it and how technology can help. In D. Nix & R. Sprio (Eds.), *Cognition, Education, & Multimedia.* Erlbaum Associates.

Brar, J., Kalbfleisch, M.L., Chandrasekher, L., Warburton, S.M., Girton, L.E., Hailyu, A., Wolfe, A., Mease, E., Mbwana, J.S., Gaillaird, W.D., & VanMeter, J.W. (2009). *Differences in Response Conflict in Autism Spectrum Disorders.* Organization of Human Brain Mapping, San Francisco, CA.

Bratman, G. N., Hamilton, J. P., Hahn, K. S., Daily, G. C., & Gross, J. J. (2015). Nature experience reduces rumination and subgenual prefrontal cortex activation. *Proceedings of the National Academy of Sciences, 112*(28), 8567–8572.

Brown, D. K., Barton, J. L., & Gladwell, V. F. (2013). Viewing nature scenes positively affects recovery of autonomic function following acute-mental stress. *Environmental Science & Technology, 47*(11), 5562–5569.

Buckner, R. L. (2010). The role of the hippocampus in prediction and imagination. *Annual Review of Psychology, 61,* 27–48.

Buckner, R. L., & Carroll, D. C. (2007). Self-projection and the brain. *Trends in Cognitive Sciences, 11*(2), 49–57. Cambridge University Press.

Bull, R., Espy, K. A., & Wiebe, S. A. (2008). Short-term memory, working memory, and executive functioning in preschoolers: Longitudinal predictors of mathematical achievement at age 7 years. *Developmental Neuropsychology, 33*(3), 205–228.

Burwell, R. A., & Shirk, S. R. (2007). Subtypes of rumination in adolescence: Associations between brooding, reflection, depressive symptoms, and coping. *Journal of Clinical Child and Adolescent Psychology, 36*(1), 56–65.

Butzlaff, R. (2000). Can music be used to teach reading? *Journal of Aesthetic Education, 34*(3/4), 167–178.

Calkins, S. D., & Williford, A. P. (2009). *Taming the terrible twos: Self-regulation and school readiness.* In O. A. Barbarin & B. H. Wasik (Eds.),

Handbook of child development and early education: Research to practice (pp. 172–198). Guilford Press.

Carlson, S. M., Moses, L. J., & Claxton, L. J. (2004). Individual differences in executive functioning and theory of mind: An investigation of inhibitory control and planning ability. *Journal of Experimental Child Psychology, 87*(4), 299–319.

Carpenter, S. K., Pashler, H., & Cepeda, N. J. (2009). Using tests to enhance 8th grade students' retention of US history facts. *Applied Cognitive Psychology: The Official Journal of the Society for Applied Research in Memory and Cognition, 23*(6), 760–771.

Carpenter, S. K., Cepeda, N. J., Rohrer, D., Kang, S. H., & Pashler, H. (2012). Using spacing to enhance diverse forms of learning: Review of recent research and implications for instruction. *Educational Psychology Review, 24*(3), 369–378.

Carr, K. W., White-Schwoch, T., Tierney, A. T., Strait, D. L., & Kraus, N. (2014). Beat synchronization predicts neural speech encoding and reading readiness in preschoolers. *Proceedings of the National Academy of Sciences, 111*(40), 14559–14564.

Cepeda, N. J., Vul, E., Rohrer, D., Wixted, J. T., & Pashler, H. (2008). Spacing effects in learning: A temporal ridgeline of optimal retention. *Psychological Science, 19*(11), 1095–1102.

Chanda, M. L., & Levitin, D. J. (2013). The neurochemistry of music. *Trends in Cognitive Sciences, 17*(4), 179–193.

Chang, T. T., Lung, T. C., Ng, C. T., & Metcalfe, A. W. (2019). Fronto-insular-parietal network engagement underlying arithmetic word problem solving. *Human Brain Mapping, 40*(6), 1927–1941.

Chiesa, A., Brambilla, P., & Serretti, A. (2010). Functional neural correlates of mindfulness meditations in comparison with psychotherapy, pharmacotherapy and placebo effect. Is there a link?. *Acta Neuropsychiatrica, 22*(3), 104–117.

Ciarocco, N. J., Vohs, K. D., & Baumeister, R. F. (2010). Some good news about rumination: Task-focused thinking after failure facilitates performance improvement. *Journal of Social and Clinical Psychology, 29*(10), 1057–1073.

Clark, C. A., Pritchard, V. E., & Woodward, L. J. (2010). Preschool executive functioning abilities predict early mathematics achievement. *Developmental Psychology, 46*(5), 1176.

Clarke, P. (1984). What Kind of Discipline Is Most Likely to Lead to Empathic Behaviour in Classrooms? *History and Social Science Teacher, 19*(4), 240–241.

Clayton, M. (2012). What is entrainment? Definition and applications in musical research. *Empirical Musicology Review, 7*(1–2), 49–56.

Cohen, S., Kamarck, T., & Mermelstein, R. (1983). A global measure of perceived stress. *Journal of Health and Social Behavior*, 385–396.

Cotton, K. (1992). *Developing empathy in children and youth*. Northwest Regional Educational Laboratory.

Cowan, N. (2000). The magical number 4 in short-term memory: A reconsideration of mental storage capacity. *Behavioral and Brain Sciences, 24*(1), 87–185.

Craig, A. (2009). How do you feel—now? The anterior insula and human awareness. *Nature Reviews Neuroscience, 10*, 59–70. https://doi.org/10.1038/nrn2555

Cragg, L., & Chevalier, N. (2012). The processes underlying flexibility in childhood. *Quarterly Journal of Experimental Psychology, 65*(2), 209–232.

Cragg, L., & Nation, K. (2009). Shifting development in mid-childhood: The influence of between-task interference. *Developmental Psychology, 45*(5), 1465.

Creswell, J. D., Taren, A. A., Lindsay, E. K., Greco, C. M., Gianaros, P. J., Fairgrieve, A., Marsland, A. L., Warren Brown, K., Way, B. M., Rosen, R. K., & Ferris, J. L. (2016). Alterations in resting-state functional connectivity link mindfulness meditation with reduced interleukin-6: a randomized controlled trial. *Biological Psychiatry, 80*(1), 53–61.

Csikzentmihalyi, M. (1990). *Flow: The psychology of optimal experience* (Vol. 1990). New York: Harper & Row.

Csikszentmihalyi, M. (2014). Toward a psychology of optimal experience. In *Flow and the foundations of positive psychology* (pp. 209–226). Springer, Dordrecht.

Dahl, R. E., & Gunnar, M. R. (2009). Heightened stress responsiveness and emotional reactivity during pubertal maturation: implications for psychopathology. *Development and psychopathology, 21*(1), 1–6.

Davidson, F., Cherry, K., & Corkum, P. (2016). Validating the behavior rating inventory of executive functioning for children with ADHD and their typically developing peers. *Applied Neuropsychology: Child, 5*(2), 127–137.

Davidson, R. J., Jackson, D. C., & Kalin, N. H. (2000). Emotion, plasticity, context, and regulation: Perspectives from affective neuroscience. *Psychological Bulletin, 126*(6), 890.

Davidson, R. J., Kabat-Zinn, J., Schumacher, J., Rosenkranz, M., Muller, D., Santorelli, S. F., Urbanowski, F., Harrington, A., Bonus, K., & Sheridan, J. F. (2003). Alterations in brain and immune function produced by mindfulness meditation. *Psychosomatic Medicine, 65*(4), 564–570.

De Waal, F. B. (2008). Putting the altruism back into altruism: The evolution of empathy. *Annual Review of Psychology, 59,* 279–300.

Diamond, M. C., Law, F., Rhodes, H., Lindner, B., Rosenzweig, M. R., Krech, D., & Bennett, E. L. (1966a). Increases in cortical depth and glia numbers in rats subjected to enriched environment. *Journal of Comparative Neurology, 128*(1), 117–125.

Diamond, M. C., Law, F., Rhodes, H., Lindner, B., Rosenzweig, M. R., Krech, D., & Bennett, E. L. (1966b). Increases in cortical depth and glia numbers in rats subjected to enriched environment. *Journal of Comparative Neurology, 128*(1), 117–125.

Dikker, S. (2019). Brain-to-brain synchrony and learning outcomes vary by student–teacher dynamics: Evidence from a real-world classroom electroencephalography study. *Journal of Cognitive Neuroscience, 31*(3), 401–411.

Dikker, S., Wan, L., Davidesco, I., Kaggen, L., Oostrik, M., McClintock, J., Rowland, J., Michalareas, G., Van Bavel, J. J., Ding, M., & Poeppel, D. (2017). Brain-to-brain synchrony tracks real-world dynamic group interactions in the classroom. *Current Biology, 27*(9), 1375–1380.

Duncan, T. A. (2013). Differentiated contracts: Giving students freedom to learn. *Kappa Delta Pi Record, 49*(4), 174–179.

Durlak, J. A., Weissberg, R. P., Dymnicki, A. B., Taylor, R. D., & Schellinger, K. B. (2011). The impact of enhancing students' social and emotional learning: A meta-analysis of school-based universal interventions. *Child Development, 82*(1), 405–432.

Düzel, E., Bunzeck, N., Guitart-Masip, M., & Düzel, S. (2010). Novelty-related motivation of anticipation and exploration by dopamine

(NOMAD): Implications for healthy aging. *Neuroscience & Biobehavioral Reviews, 34*(5), 660–669.

Dweck, C. S. (2008). *Mindset: The new psychology of success*. Random House Digital, Inc.

Dweck, C. S. (2014). Mindsets and math/science achievement. Carnegie Corporation of New York-Institute for Advanced Study Commission on Mathematics and Science Education.

Dyrda, B. (2009). The process of diagnosing the underachievement syndrome in gifted and creative children. *The New Educational Review, 18*(2), 129–137.Dyregrov, A., & Yule, W. (2006). A review of PTSD in children. *Child and Adolescent Mental Health, 11*(4), 176–184.

Eichele, T., Debener, S., Calhoun, V. D., Specht, K., Engel, A. K., Hugdahl, K., . . . & Ullsperger, M. (2008). Prediction of human errors by maladaptive changes in event-related brain networks. *Proceedings of the National Academy of Sciences, 105*(16), 6173–6178.

Eide, B., & Eide, F. (2012). *The dyslexic advantage: Unlocking the hidden potential of the dyslexic brain*. Penguin.

Eisenberger, N. I., & Cole, S. W. (2012). Social neuroscience and health: neurophysiological mechanisms linking social ties with physical health. *Nature Neuroscience, 15*(5), 669–674.

Engel-Yeger, B., Muzio, C., Rinosi, G., Solano, P., Geoffroy, P. A., Pompili, M., . . . & Serafini, G. (2016). Extreme sensory processing patterns and their relation with clinical conditions among individuals with major affective disorders. *Psychiatry Research, 236,* 112–118.

Engemann, K., Pedersen, C. B., Arge, L., Tsirogiannis, C., Mortensen, P. B., & Svenning, J. C. (2019). Residential green space in childhood is associated with lower risk of psychiatric disorders from adolescence into adulthood. *Proceedings of the National Academy of Sciences, 116*(11), 5188–5193.

Ericsson, K. A., Krampe, R. T., & Tesch-Römer, C. (1993). The role of deliberate practice in the acquisition of expert performance. *Psychological Review, 100*(3), 363.

Eriksen, B. A., & Eriksen, C. W. (1974). Effects of noise letters upon the identification of a target letter in a nonsearch task. *Perception & Psychophysics, 16*(1), 143–149.

Feldman, A., & Minstrell, J. (2000). *Action research as a research methodology for the study of the teaching and learning of science.* ERIC Clearinghouse.

Feng, K., Zhao, X., Liu, J., Cai, Y., Ye, Z., Chen, C., & Xue, G. (2019). Spaced learning enhances episodic memory by increasing neural pattern similarity across repetitions. *Journal of Neuroscience, 39*(27), 5351–5360.

Feshbach, N. D., & Feshbach, S. (2009). Empathy and education. *The Social Neuroscience of Empathy, 85,* 98.

Flook, L., Goldberg, S. B., Pinger, L., & Davidson, R. J. (2015). Promoting prosocial behavior and self-regulatory skills in preschool children through a mindfulness-based kindness curriculum. *Developmental Psychology, 51*(1), 44.

Fox, K. C., & Christoff, K. (Eds.). (2018). *The Oxford handbook of spontaneous thought: Mind-wandering, creativity, and dreaming.* Oxford University Press.

Fredrickson, B. L. (2004). The broaden–and–build theory of positive emotions. *Philosophical Transactions of the Royal Society of London. Series B: Biological Sciences, 359*(1449), 1367–1377.

Fredrickson, B. L. (2013). Positive emotions broaden and build. In P. Devine & A. Plant (Eds.), *Advances in Experimental Social Psychology* (Vol. 47, pp. 1–53). Academic Press.

Galante, J., Galante, I., Bekkers, M. J., & Gallacher, J. (2014). Effect of kindness-based meditation on health and well-being: A systematic review and meta-analysis. *Journal of Consulting and Clinical Psychology, 82*(6), 1101.

Garland, E. L., Fredrickson, B., Kring, A. M., Johnson, D. P., Meyer, P. S., & Penn, D. L. (2010). Upward spirals of positive emotions counter downward spirals of negativity: Insights from the broaden-and-build theory and affective neuroscience on the treatment of emotion dysfunctions and deficits in psychopathology. *Clinical Psychology Review, 30*(7), 849–864.

Garrison, K. A., Zeffiro, T. A., Scheinost, D., Constable, R. T., & Brewer, J. A. (2015). Meditation leads to reduced default mode network activity beyond an active task. *Cognitive, Affective, & Behavioral Neuroscience, 15*(3), 712–720.

Geary, D. C. (2011). Cognitive predictors of achievement growth in mathematics: A 5-year longitudinal study. *Developmental Psychology, 47*(6), 1539.

Gerhart, B., & Fang, M. (2015). Pay, intrinsic motivation, extrinsic motivation, performance, and creativity in the workplace: Revisiting long-held beliefs. *Annual Review of Organizational Psychology and Organizational Behavior, 2,* 489–521.

Gobet, F., Lane, P. C., Croker, S., Cheng, P. C., Jones, G., Oliver, I., & Pine, J. M. (2001). Chunking mechanisms in human learning. *Trends in Cognitive Sciences, 5*(6), 236–243.

Goldsmith, H. H., & Davidson, R. J. (2004). Disambiguating the components of emotion regulation. *Child Development, 75*(2), 361–365.Gonzalez, A. A. (2019, January 18). What Happens When Meditation Replaces Detention. *Our Children.* https://ptaourchildren.org/meditation-not-detention/

Green, L. W. (2008). Making research relevant: if it is an evidence-based practice, where's the practice-based evidence?. *Family practice, 25*(suppl_1), i20–i24.

Gülgöz, S., & Gelman, S. A. (2017). Who's the boss? Concepts of social power across development. *Child Development, 88*(3), 946–963.

Hanoch, Y., & Vitouch, O. (2004). When less is more: Information, emotional arousal and the ecological reframing of the Yerkes-Dodson law. *Theory & Psychology, 14*(4), 427–452.

Hannon, E. E., & Johnson, S. P. (2005). Infants use meter to categorize rhythms and melodies: Implications for musical structure learning. *Cognitive Psychology, 50*(4), 354–377.

Happé, F., & Frith, U. (2006). The weak coherence account: detail-focused cognitive style in autism spectrum disorders. *Journal of Autism and Developmental Disorders, 36*(1), 5–25.

Heim, C., & Binder, E. B. (2012). Current research trends in early life stress and depression: Review of human studies on sensitive periods, gene–environment interactions, and epigenetics. *Experimental Neurology, 233*(1), 102–111.

Heitz, R. P., & Engle, R. W. (2007). Focusing the spotlight: Individual differences in visual attention control. *Journal of Experimental Psychology: General, 136*(2), 217.

Heitz, R. P., Schrock, J. C., Payne, T. W., & Engle, R. W. (2008). Effects of incentive on working memory capacity: Behavioral and pupillometric data. *Psychophysiology, 45*(1), 119–129.

Herbert, B., & Anderson, K. J. (2003). *Dune: House Harkonnen* (Vol. 2). Spectra.

Hill, E. L. (2004). Executive dysfunction in autism. *Trends in cognitive sciences, 8*(1), 26–32.

Hinshaw, S. P. (1992). Externalizing behavior problems and academic underachievement in childhood and adolescence: Causal relationships and underlying mechanisms. *Psychological bulletin, 111*(1), 127.

Hölzel, B. K., Carmody, J., Evans, K. C., Hoge, E. A., Dusek, J. A., Morgan, L., Pitman, R. K., & Lazar, S. W. (2010). Stress reduction correlates with structural changes in the amygdala. *Social Cognitive and Affective Neuroscience, 5*(1), 11–17.

Huntley, J. D., Hampshire, A., Bor, D., Owen, A., & Howard, R. J. (2017). Adaptive working memory strategy training in early Alzheimer's disease: Randomised controlled trial. *The British Journal of Psychiatry, 210*(1), 61–66.

Immordino-Yang, M. H., Christodoulou, J. A., & Singh, V. (2012). Rest is not idleness: Implications of the brain's default mode for human development and education. *Perspectives on Psychological Science, 7*(4), 352–364.

Jaekel, J., Eryigit-Madzwamuse, S., & Wolke, D. (2016). Preterm toddlers' inhibitory control abilities predict attention regulation and academic achievement at age 8 years. *The Journal of Pediatrics, 169*, 87–92.

Jahncke, H., Björkeholm, P., Marsh, J. E., Odelius, J., & Sörqvist, P. (2016). Office noise: Can headphones and masking sound attenuate distraction by background speech? *Work, 55*(3), 505–513.

Jang, J. H., Jung, W. H., Kang, D. H., Byun, M. S., Kwon, S. J., Choi, C. H., & Kwon, J. S. (2011). Increased default mode network connectivity associated with meditation. *Neuroscience Letters, 487*(3), 358–362.

Jaschke, A. C., Honing, H., & Scherder, E. J. (2018). Longitudinal analysis of music education on executive functions in primary school children. *Frontiers in Neuroscience, 12*, 103.

Kabat-Zinn, J. (2009). *Wherever you go, there you are: Mindfulness meditation in everyday life.* Hachette Books.

Kaimal, G., Ray, K., & Muniz, J. (2016). Reduction of cortisol levels and participants' responses following art making. *Art Therapy, 33*(2), 74–80.

Kalbfleisch, M. L. (2004). Functional neural anatomy of talent. *The Anatomical Record Part B: The New Anatomist, 277B*, 21–36. https://doi.org/10.1002/ar.b.20010

Kalbfleisch, M. L. (2008). Getting to the heart of the brain: Using cognitive neuroscience to explore the nature of human ability and performance. *Roeper Review, 30*(3), 162–170.

Kalbfleisch, M. L. (October, 2009). *Literacy, Scientific and Otherwise, the Role of Story, and the Impact of Environment on the Brain and Behavior.* FLICC Forum on Information Policies, Library of Congress, Washington, D.C.

Kalbfleisch, M. L. (2009). The neural plasticity of giftedness. In L. V. Shavinina (Ed.), *International handbook on giftedness* (pp. 275–293). Springer.

Kalbfleisch, M. L. (2012). Twice Exceptional Students. In C. A. Callahan & H. Hertberg- Davis (Eds.), *Fundamentals of Gifted Education: Considering Multiple Perspectives* (pp. 358–368). Routledge.

Kalbfleisch, M. L., & Loughan, A. R. (2012). Impact of IQ discrepancy on executive function in high-functioning autism: Insight into twice exceptionality. *Journal of Autism and Developmental Disorders, 42*(3), 390–400.

Kalbfleisch, M.L. (2013). Twice Exceptional Learners. In J. A. Plucker & C. M. Callahan (Eds.), *Critical Issues and Practices in Gifted Education* (2nd ed., pp. 269–287). Prufrock Press.

Kalbfleisch, M. L. (2017). Neurodevelopment of the executive functions. In E. Goldberg (Ed.), *Executive Functions in Health and Disease* (pp. 143–167). Elsevier.

Kalbfleisch, M. L., de Bettencourt, M. T., Kopperman, R., Banasiak, M., Roberts, J. M., & Halavi, M. (2013). Environmental influences on neural systems of relational complexity. *Frontiers in Psychology, 4*, 631. https://doi.org/10.3389/fpsyg.2013.00631

Kalbfleisch, M. L., Van Meter, J. W., & Zeffiro, T. A. (2007). The influences of task difficulty and response correctness on neural systems supporting fluid reasoning. *Cognitive Neurodynamics, 1*(1), 71–84. https://doi.org/10.1007/s11571-006-9007-4

Kane, M. J., & Engle, R. W. (2002). The role of prefrontal cortex in working-memory capacity, executive attention, and general fluid intelligence: An individual-differences perspective. *Psychonomic Bulletin & Review, 9*(4), 637–671.

Kane, M. J., & McVay, J. C. (2012). What mind wandering reveals about executive-control abilities and failures. *Current Directions in Psychological Science, 21*(5), 348–354.

Kaufmann, F., Kalbfleisch, M.L., & Castellanos, F.X. (2000). *Attention Deficit Disorders and Gifted Students: What Do We Really Know?* Monograph: National Research Center on the Gifted and Talented. University of Connecticut, Storrs, CT.

Kelley, P., & Whatson, T. (2013). Making long-term memories in minutes: A spaced learning pattern from memory research in education. *Frontiers in Human Neuroscience, 7,* 589.

Khalil, A. K., Minces, V., McLoughlin, G., & Chiba, A. (2013). Group rhythmic synchrony and attention in children. *Frontiers in Psychology, 4,* 564.

Killingsworth, M. A., & Gilbert, D. T. (2010). A wandering mind is an unhappy mind. *Science, 330*(6006), 932–932.

King, A. (1990). Enhancing peer interaction and learning in the classroom through reciprocal questioning. *American Educational Research Journal, 27*(4), 664–687.

Kirschner, S., & Tomasello, M. (2010). Joint music making promotes prosocial behavior in 4-year-old children. *Evolution and Human Behavior, 31*(5), 354–364.

Knoblich, G., Butterfill, S., & Sebanz, N. (2011). Psychological research on joint action: Theory and data. In B. Ross (Ed.), *Psychology of learning and motivation* (Vol. 54, pp. 59–101). Academic Press.

Koelsch, S. (2010). Towards a neural basis of music-evoked emotions. *Trends in Cognitive Sciences, 14*(3), 131–137.

Koelsch, S., Fritz, T., v. Cramon, D. Y., Müller, K., & Friederici, A. D. (2006). Investigating emotion with music: an fMRI study. *Human brain mapping, 27*(3), 239–250.

Koike, T., Tanabe, H. C., Okazaki, S., Nakagawa, E., Sasaki, A. T., Shimada, K., Sugawara, S. K., Takahashi, H. K., Yoshihara, K., Bosch-Bayard, J., & Sadato, N. (2016). Neural substrates of shared attention as social memory: A hyperscanning functional magnetic resonance imaging study. *Neuroimage, 125,* 401–412.

Komarraju, M., & Nadler, D. (2013). Self-efficacy and academic achievement: Why do implicit beliefs, goals, and effort regulation matter?. *Learning and individual differences, 25,* 67–72.

Kraus, N., & White-Schwoch, T. (2020). The Argument for Music Education. *American Scientist, 108*(4), 210–213.

Kuhl, P. K. (2010). Brain mechanisms in early language acquisition. *Neuron, 67*(5), 713–727.

Lai, M. C., Lombardo, M. V., Ruigrok, A. N., Chakrabarti, B., Auyeung, B., Szatmari, P., . . . & MRC AIMS Consortium. (2017). Quantifying and exploring camouflaging in men and women with autism. *Autism, 21*(6), 690–702.

Lambert, S., Sampaio, E., Mauss, Y., & Scheiber, C. (2004). Blindness and brain plasticity: contribution of mental imagery?: an fMRI study. *Cognitive Brain Research, 20*(1), 1–11.

Le Bouc, R., & Pessiglione, M. (2013). Imaging social motivation: Distinct brain mechanisms drive effort production during collaboration versus competition. *Journal of Neuroscience, 33*(40), 15894–15902.

Lemieux, C. M. (2001). Learning contracts in the classroom: Tools for empowerment and accountability. *Social work education, 20*(2), 263–276.

Lewis, M. D. (2005). Self-organizing individual differences in brain development. *Developmental Review, 25*(3–4), 252–277.

Lindenberger, U., Li, S. C., Gruber, W., & Müller, V. (2009). Brains swinging in concert: Cortical phase synchronization while playing guitar. *BMC neuroscience, 10*(1), 22.

Lindquist, K. A., Barrett, L. F., Bliss-Moreau, E., & Russell, J. A. (2006). Language and the perception of emotion. *Emotion, 6*(1), 125.

Lindquist, S. I., & McLean, J. P. (2011). Daydreaming and its correlates in an educational environment. *Learning and Individual Differences, 21*(2), 158–167.

Linnavalli, T., Putkinen, V., Lipsanen, J., Huotilainen, M., & Tervaniemi, M. (2018). Music playschool enhances children's linguistic skills. *Scientific Reports, 8*(1), 1–10.

Luciana, M., Collins, P. F., Olson, E. A., & Schissel, A. M. (2009). Tower of London performance in healthy adolescents: The development of planning skills and associations with self-reported inattention and impulsivity. *Developmental Neuropsychology, 34*(4), 461–475.Luck, S. J. & Vogel, E. K. (1997). The capacity of visual working memory for features and conjunctions. *Nature, 390,* 279–281.

Ludlow, A., Mohr, B., Whitmore, A., Garagnani, M., Pulvermüller, F., &

Gutierrez, R. (2014). Auditory processing and sensory behaviours in children with autism spectrum disorders as revealed by mismatch negativity. *Brain and Cognition, 86,* 55–63.

Lundbye-Jensen, J., Skriver, K., Nielsen, J. B., & Roig, M. (2017). Acute exercise improves motor memory consolidation in preadolescent children. *Frontiers in Human Neuroscience, 11,* 182.

Lutz, A., Brefczynski-Lewis, J., Johnstone, T., & Davidson, R. J. (2008). Regulation of the neural circuitry of emotion by compassion meditation: effects of meditative expertise. *PloS one, 3*(3), e1897.

Maenner, M. J., Shaw, K. A., & Baio, J. (2020). Prevalence of autism spectrum disorder among children aged 8 years—autism and developmental disabilities monitoring network, 11 sites, United States, 2016. *MMWR Surveillance Summaries, 69*(4), 1.

Mar, R. A., Oatley, K., & Peterson, J. B. (2009). Exploring the link between reading fiction and empathy: Ruling out individual differences and examining outcomes. *Communications, 34*(4), 407–428.

Mascaro, J. S., Darcher, A., Negi, L. T., & Raison, C. L. (2015). The neural mediators of kindness-based meditation: a theoretical model. *Frontiers in Psychology, 6,* 109.

Mathews, A., Ridgeway, V., & Holmes, E. A. (2013). Feels like the real thing: Imagery is both more realistic and emotional than verbal thought. *Cognition & Emotion, 27*(2), 217–229.

Mathy, F., & Feldman, J. (2012). What's magic about magic numbers? Chunking and data compression in short-term memory. *Cognition, 122*(3), 346–362.

Matthews, S. G., & Phillips, D. I. (2012). Transgenerational inheritance of stress pathology. *Experimental Neurology, 233*(1), 95–101.

Mauduit, A. (April 26, 2016). Teaching high-academic level classes throughout art. *LinkedIn.*

https://www.linkedin.com/pulse/teaching-high-academic-level-classes -throughout-art-adrien-mauduit/?trackingId=

Mayes, S. D., & Calhoun, S. L. (2007). Learning, attention, writing, and processing speed in typical children and children with ADHD, autism, anxiety, depression, and oppositional-defiant disorder. *Child Neuropsychology, 13*(6), 469–493.

McAlonan, G. M., Cheung, C., Cheung, V., Wong, N., Suckling, J., &

Chua, S. E. (2009). Differential effects on white-matter systems in high-functioning autism and Asperger's syndrome. *Psychological Medicine, 39*(11), 1885–1893.

McClelland, M. M., Cameron, C. E., Duncan, R., Bowles, R. P., Acock, A. C., Miao, A., & Pratt, M. E. (2014). Predictors of early growth in academic achievement: The head-toes-knees-shoulders task. *Frontiers in Psychology, 5*, 599.

McMahan, E. A., & Estes, D. (2015). The effect of contact with natural environments on positive and negative affect: A meta-analysis. *The Journal of Positive Psychology, 10*(6), 507–519.

McVay, J. C., & Kane, M. J. (2009). Conducting the train of thought: working memory capacity, goal neglect, and mind wandering in an executive-control task. *Journal of Experimental Psychology: Learning, Memory, and Cognition, 35*(1), 196.

McVay, J. C., & Kane, M. J. (2012). Why does working memory capacity predict variation in reading comprehension? On the influence of mind wandering and executive attention. *Journal of experimental psychology: general, 141*(2), 302.

Mercier, C., & Sirigu, A. (2009). Training with virtual visual feedback to alleviate phantom limb pain. *Neurorehabilitation and Neural Repair, 23*(6), 587–594.

Miendlarzewska, E. A., & Trost, W. J. (2014). How musical training affects cognitive development: Rhythm, reward and other modulating variables. *Frontiers in neuroscience, 7*, 279.

Miller, G. A. (1956). The magical number seven, plus or minus two: Some limits on our capacity for processing information. *Psychological review, 63*(2), 81.

Mills, G. E. (2000). *Action research: A guide for the teacher researcher.* Prentice Hall.

Mills, K. L., Goddings, A. L., Herting, M. M., Meuwese, R., Blakemore, S. J., Crone, E. A., . . . & Tamnes, C. K. (2016). Structural brain development between childhood and adulthood: Convergence across four longitudinal samples. *Neuroimage, 141*, 273–281.

Miranda, A., Berenguer, C., Roselló, B., Baixauli, I., & Colomer, C. (2017). Social cognition in children with high-functioning autism spectrum disorder and attention-deficit/hyperactivity disorder. Associations with executive functions. *Frontiers in Psychology, 8,* 1035.

Miyake, A., & Friedman, N. P. (1998). Individual differences in second language proficiency: Working memory as language aptitude. *Foreign Language learning: Psycholinguistic studies on training and retention,* 339–364.

Miyake, A., Friedman, N. P., Emerson, M. J., Witzki, A. H., Howerter, A., & Wager, T. D. (2000). The unity and diversity of executive functions and their contributions to complex "frontal lobe" tasks: A latent variable analysis. *Cognitive Psychology, 41*(1), 49–100.

Moore, A., & Malinowski, P. (2009). Meditation, mindfulness and cognitive flexibility. *Consciousness and cognition, 18*(1), 176–186.

Moreno, S., Bialystok, E., Barac, R., Schellenberg, E. G., Cepeda, N. J., & Chau, T. (2011). Short-term music training enhances verbal intelligence and executive function. *Psychological science, 22*(11), 1425–1433.

Morgan, P. L., Farkas, G., Wang, Y., Hillemeier, M. M., Oh, Y., & Maczuga, S. (2019). Executive function deficits in kindergarten predict repeated academic difficulties across elementary school. *Early Childhood Research Quarterly, 46,* 20–32.

Morrison, F. J., Ponitz, C. C., & McClelland, M. M. (2010). Self-regulation and academic achievement in the transition to school.

Mrazek, M. D., Smallwood, J., & Schooler, J. W. (2012). Mindfulness and mind-wandering: Finding convergence through opposing constructs. *Emotion, 12*(3), 442.

Munby, H., & Russell, T. (1990). Metaphor in the study of teachers' professional knowledge. *Theory into practice, 29*(2), 116–121.

Mundy, P., & Newell, L. (2007). Attention, joint attention, and social cognition. *Current directions in psychological science, 16*(5), 269–274.

Nassar, M. R., McGuire, J. T., Ritz, H., & Kable, J. W. (2019). Dissociable forms of uncertainty-driven representational change across the human brain. *Journal of Neuroscience, 39*(9), 1688–1698.

Nation, K. (1999). Reading skills in hyperlexia: A developmental perspective. *Psychological bulletin, 125*(3), 338.

Oakes, J. (1990). *Multiplying inequalities: The effects of race, social class, and tracking on opportunities to learn mathematics and science.* Rand Corporation, Santa Monica, CA.

Olff, M., Frijling, J. L., Kubzansky, L. D., Bradley, B., Ellenbogen, M. A., Cardoso, C., Bartz J.A., Yee, J.R., & Van Zuiden, M. (2013). The role of oxytocin in social bonding, stress regulation and mental health: An update on the moderating effects of context and interindividual differences. *Psychoneuroendocrinology, 38*(9), 1883–1894.Opai, K. (2017). A time and space for takiwātanga. *Altogether Autism Takiwtānga.*

Osaka, N., Minamoto, T., Yaoi, K., Azuma, M., & Osaka, M. (2014). Neural synchronization during cooperated humming: a hyperscanning study using fNIRS. *Procedia-Social and Behavioral Sciences, 126,* 241–243.

Paparella, T., & Freeman, S. F. (2015). Methods to improve joint attention in young children with autism: A review. *Pediatric health, medicine, and therapeutics, 6,* 65.

Paraskevas, A., & Wickens, E. (2003). Andragogy and the Socratic method: The adult learner perspective. *Journal of Hospitality, Leisure, Sport, & Tourism Education, 2*(2), 4–14.

Pashler, H., Bain, P., Bottge, B., Graesser, A., Koedinger, K., McDaniel, M., & Metcalfe, J. (2007). *Organizing instruction and study to improve student learning (NCER 2007- 2004).* National Center for Education Research.

Passolunghi, M. C., & Siegel, L. S. (2001). Short-term memory, working memory, and inhibitory control in children with difficulties in arithmetic problem solving. *Journal of Experimental child psychology, 80*(1), 44–57.

Pearson, J. (2019). The human imagination: The cognitive neuroscience of visual mental imagery. *Nature Reviews Neuroscience, 20*(10), 624–634.

Pearson, J., Naselaris, T., Holmes, E. A., & Kosslyn, S. M. (2015). Mental imagery: Functional mechanisms and clinical applications. *Trends in Cognitive Sciences, 19*(10), 590–602.

Pellis, S. M., Pellis, V. C., & Bell, H. C. (2010). The function of play in the development of the social brain. *American Journal of Play, 2*(3), 278–296.Pennington, B. F., & Olson, R. K. (2005). *Genetics of Dyslexia.* In M. J. Snowling & C. Hulme (Eds.), *Blackwell handbooks of developmental psychology. The science of reading: A handbook* (p. 453–472). Blackwell Publishing.

Pesce, C., Crova, C., Cereatti, L., Casella, R., & Bellucci, M. (2009). Physical activity and mental performance in preadolescents: Effects of acute exercise on free-recall memory. *Mental Health and Physical Activity, 2*(1), 16–22.

Pessoa, L., Lindquist, K. A., Wager, T. D., Kober, H., Bliss-Moreau, E., & Barrett, L. F. (2012). Beyond brain regions: Network perspective of cognition–emotion interactions. *Behavioral and Brain Sciences, 35*(3), 158.

Prabhakaran, V., Rypma, B., Narayanan, N. S., Meier, T. B., Austin, B. P., Nair, V. A., Naing, L., Thomas, L.E., & Gabrieli, J. D. (2011). Capacity-speed relationships in prefrontal cortex. *PLoS One, 6*(11).

Prast, E. J., Weijer-Bergsma, E., Kroesbergen, E. H., & Van Luit, J. E. (2015). Readiness-based differentiation in primary school mathematics: Expert recommendations and teacher self-assessment. *Frontline Learning Research, 3*(2), 90–116.

Rademacher, L., Schulte-Rüther, M., Hanewald, B., & Lammertz, S. (2015). Reward: from basic reinforcers to anticipation of social cues. In M. Wöhr & S. Krach (Eds.) *Social Behavior from Rodents to Humans* (pp. 207–221). Springer.

Ramachandran, V. S., & Hirstein, W. (1998). The perception of phantom limbs. The DO Hebb lecture. *Brain: a journal of neurology, 121*(9), 1603–1630.

Ramachandran, V. S., & Rogers-Ramachandran, D. (2000). Phantom limbs and neural plasticity. *Archives of neurology, 57*(3), 317–320.

Rea, C. P., & Modigliani, V. (1985). The effect of expanded versus massed practice on the retention of multiplication facts and spelling lists. *Human Learning: Journal of Practical Research & Applications.*

Redcay, E., Dodell-Feder, D., Pearrow, M. J., Mavros, P. L., Kleiner, M., Gabrieli, J. D., & Saxe, R. (2010). Live face-to-face interaction during fMRI: a new tool for social cognitive neuroscience. *Neuroimage, 50*(4), 1639–1647.

Reynolds, S. M., & Berridge, K. C. (2008). Emotional environments retune the valence of appetitive versus fearful functions in nucleus accumbens. *Nature neuroscience, 11*(4), 423–425.

Ritter, S. M., Damian, R. I., Simonton, D. K., van Baaren, R. B., Strick, M., Derks, J., & Dijksterhuis, A. (2012). Diversifying experiences enhance cognitive flexibility. *Journal of experimental social psychology, 48*(4), 961–964.

Roberts, J. M. (2014). *The Impact of Organization Structure on Information Manipulation and Reasoning–An fMRI Study* [Doctoral dissertation, George Mason University].

Roberts, R. P., Wiebels, K., Sumner, R. L., van Mulukom, V., Grady, C. L., Schacter, D. L., & Addis, D. R. (2017). An fMRI investigation of the relationship between future imagination and cognitive flexibility. *Neuropsychologia, 95*, 156–172.

Robertson, J. (2000). The three Rs of action research methodology: reciprocity, reflexivity, and reflection-on-reality. *Educational action research, 8*(2), 307–326.

Roden, I., Grube, D., Bongard, S., & Kreutz, G. (2014). Does music training enhance working memory performance? Findings from a quasi-experimental longitudinal study. *Psychology of Music, 42*(2), 284–298.

Röer, J. P., Bell, R., & Buchner, A. (2014). Please silence your cell phone: Your ringtone captures other people's attention. *Noise and health, 16*(68), 34.

Rohrer, D., & Taylor, K. (2006). The effects of overlearning and distributed practise on the retention of mathematics knowledge. *Applied Cognitive Psychology: The Official Journal of the Society for Applied Research in Memory and Cognition, 20*(9), 1209–1224.

Rose, S. A., Feldman, J. F., & Jankowski, J. J. (2011). Modeling a cascade of effects: The role of speed and executive functioning in preterm/full-term differences in academic achievement. *Developmental Science, 14*(5), 1161–1175.

Rothbaum, F., & Trommsdorff, G. (2007). *Do Roots and Wings Complement or Oppose One Another? The Socialization of Relatedness and Autonomy in Cultural Context.* Guilford press.

Roubinov, D. S., Boyce, W. T., Lee, M. R., & Bush, N. R. (2020). Evidence for discrete profiles of children's physiological activity across three neurobiological system and their transitions over time. *Developmental Science*, e12989.

Rowe, G., Hirsh, J. B., & Anderson, A. K. (2007). Positive affect increases the breadth of attentional selection. *Proceedings of the National Academy of Sciences, 104*(1), 383–388.

Rueda, M. R., Posner, M. I., & Rothbart, M. K. (2005). The development of executive attention: Contributions to the emergence of self-regulation. *Developmental neuropsychology, 28*(2), 573–594.

Sabol, T. J., Bohlmann, N. L., & Downer, J. T. (2018). Low-income ethnically diverse children's engagement as a predictor of school readiness above preschool classroom quality. *Child development, 89*(2), 556–576.

Sacks, O. (1973). *Awakenings.* Duckworth & Co.

Sacks, O. (1985). *The Man Who Mistook His Wife for a Hat.* Summit Books.

Sacks, O. (1995). *An Anthropologist on Mars.* Alfred A. Knopf.

Sacks, O. (1997, May 26). Water Babies. *The New Yorker.* https://www.newyorker.com/magazine/1997/05/26/water-babies

Sacks, O. (2007). *Musicophilia: Tales of Music and the Brain.* Alfred A. Knopf.

Sahyoun, C. P., Belliveau, J. W., Soulières, I., Schwartz, S., & Mody, M. (2010). Neuroimaging of the functional and structural networks underlying visuospatial vs. linguistic reasoning in high-functioning autism. *Neuropsychologia, 48*(1), 86–95.

Salas, E., Sims, D. E., & Burke, C. S. (2005). Is there a "big five" in teamwork? *Small group research, 36*(5), 555–599.

Sänger, J., Müller, V., & Lindenberger, U. (2012). Intra- and interbrain synchronization and network properties when playing guitar in duets. *Frontiers in human neuroscience, 6*, 312.

Saxe, R., Tenenbaum, J. B., & Carey, S. (2005). Secret agents: Inferences about hidden causes by 10-and 12-month-old infants. *Psychological Science, 16*(12), 995–1001.

Schilbach, L., Timmermans, B., Reddy, V., Costall, A., Bente, G., Schlicht, T., & Vogeley, K. (2013). Toward a second-person neuroscience. *Behavioral and brain sciences, 36*(4), 393–414.

Schmitz, T. W., De Rosa, E., & Anderson, A. K. (2009). Opposing influences of affective state valence on visual cortical encoding. *Journal of Neuroscience, 29*(22), 7199–7207.

Schomaker, J., & Meeter, M. (2015). Short- and long-lasting consequences of novelty, deviance, and surprise on brain and cognition. *Neuroscience & Biobehavioral Reviews, 55*, 268–279.

Sendak, M. (1963). *Where the wild things are.* Harper & Row.

Shaw, K. A., Maenner, M. J., & Baio, J. (2020). Early identification of autism spectrum disorder among children aged 4 years—Early Autism and Developmental Disabilities Monitoring Network, six sites, United States, 2016. *MMWR Surveillance Summaries, 69*(3), 1.

Shapero, B. G., McClung, G., Bangasser, D. A., Abramson, L. Y., &

Alloy, L. B. (2017). Interaction of biological stress recovery and cognitive vulnerability for depression in adolescence. *Journal of youth and adolescence, 46*(1), 91–103.

Sheikh, A. A. (Ed.). (2003). *Healing images: The role of imagination in health.* Baywood Publishing Company, Inc.

Silberman, S. (2015). *Neurotribes: The legacy of autism and the future of neurodiversity.* New York: Penguin.

Sinek, S. (2016). *Together is better: A little book of inspiration.* Penguin.

Singer, J. L. (1975). Navigating the stream of consciousness: research in daydreaming and related inner experience. *American Psychologist, 30*(7), 727.

Slater, J., Skoe, E., Strait, D. L., O'Connell, S., Thompson, E., & Kraus, N. (2015). Music training improves speech-in-noise perception: Longitudinal evidence from a community-based music program. *Behavioural brain research, 291*, 244–252.

Smallwood, J., & Schooler, J. W. (2014). Mind-wandering: The scientific navigation of the stream of consciousness. *Annual Review of Psychology, 66*, 487–518.

Smith, P., Perrin, S., Dalgleish, T., Meiser-Stedman, R., Clark, D. M., & Yule, W. (2013). Treatment of posttraumatic stress disorder in children and adolescents. *Current Opinion in Psychiatry, 26*(1), 66–72.

Smolen, P., Zhang, Y., & Byrne, J. H. (2016). The right time to learn: mechanisms and optimization of spaced learning. *Nature Reviews Neuroscience, 17*(2), 77.

Sobel, H. S., Cepeda, N. J., & Kapler, I. V. (2011). Spacing effects in real-world classroom vocabulary learning. *Applied Cognitive Psychology, 25*(5), 763–767.

Sowell, E. R., Trauner, D. A., Gamst, A., & Jernigan, T. L. (2002). Development of cortical and subcortical brain structures in childhood and adolescence: a structural MRI study. *Developmental Medicine & Child Neurology, 44*(1), 4–16.

Spelke, E. S., & Kinzler, K. D. (2007). Core knowledge. *Developmental science, 10*(1), 89–96.

Stallen, M., De Dreu, C. K., Shalvi, S., Smidts, A., & Sanfey, A. G. (2012). The herding hormone: oxytocin stimulates in-group conformity. *Psychological science, 23*(11), 1288–1292.

Starko, A. J. (2017). *Creativity in the classroom: Schools of curious delight.* Routledge.

St Clair-Thompson, H. L., & Gathercole, S. E. (2006). Executive functions and achievements in school: Shifting, updating, inhibition, and working memory. *Quarterly journal of experimental psychology, 59*(4), 745–759.

Stephens, G. J., Silbert, L. J., & Hasson, U. (2010). Speaker–listener neural coupling underlies successful communication. *Proceedings of the National Academy of Sciences, 107*(32), 14425–14430.

Suddendorf, T., & Corballis, M. C. (2007). The evolution of foresight: What is mental time travel, and is it unique to humans? *Behavioral and brain sciences, 30*(3), 299–313.

Supekar, K., & Menon, V. (2012). Developmental maturation of dynamic causal control signals in higher-order cognition: a neurocognitive network model. *PLoS computational biology, 8*(2).

Szpunar, K. K., Spreng, R. N., & Schacter, D. L. (2014). A taxonomy of prospection: Introducing an organizational framework for future-oriented cognition. *Proceedings of the National Academy of Sciences, 111*(52), 18414–18421.

Tabibnia, G., & Lieberman, M. D. (2007). Fairness and cooperation are rewarding: evidence from social cognitive neuroscience. *Annals of the New York Academy of Sciences, 1118*(1), 90–101.

Tang, Y. Y., Hölzel, B. K., & Posner, M. I. (2015). The neuroscience of mindfulness meditation. *Nature Reviews Neuroscience, 16*(4), 213–225.

Tang, Y. Y., Lu, Q., Fan, M., Yang, Y., & Posner, M. I. (2012). Mechanisms of white matter changes induced by meditation. *Proceedings of the National Academy of Sciences, 109*(26), 10570–10574.

Tehan, G., Arber, M., & Tolan, G. A. (2018). Working memory capacity as a determinant of proactive interference and auditory distraction. *Journal of cognition, 2*(1).

The Legacy Project: Growth Hack Your Life (2015, April 30). Joy Harjo—poet, musician, and author [Interview]. Retrieved from https://www.thelegacyproject.co.za/2015/04/30/joy-harjo-poet-musician-author/

Threadgold, E., Marsh, J. E., McLatchie, N., & Ball, L. J. (2019). Background music stints creativity: Evidence from compound remote associate tasks. *Applied Cognitive Psychology, 33*(5), 873–888.

Tierney, A., & Kraus, N. (2013a). Music training for the development of reading skills. In M. Merzenich, M. Nahum, & T. van Vleet (Eds.), *Progress in brain research* (Vol. 207, pp. 209–241). Elsevier.

Tierney, A., & Kraus, N. (2013b). The ability to move to a beat is linked to the consistency of neural responses to sound. *Journal of Neuroscience, 33*(38), 14981–14988.

Titz, C., & Karbach, J. (2014). Working memory and executive functions: effects of training on academic achievement. *Psychological research, 78*(6), 852–868.

Tolkien, J. R. R. (1954). *The Fellowship of the Ring.* George Allen & Unwin.

Tomlinson, C. A. (1995). *Differentiating instruction for advanced learners in the mixed-ability middle school classroom.* ERIC Clearinghouse on Disabilities and Gifted Education.

Tomlinson, C. A. (2000). Reconcilable differences: Standards-based teaching and differentiation. *Educational leadership, 58*(1), 6–13.

Tomlinson, C. A., & Kalbfleisch, M. L. (1998). Teach me, teach my brain: A call for differentiated classrooms. *Educational Leadership, 56*(3), 52–55.

Trehub, S. E., & Hannon, E. E. (2006). Infant music perception: Domain-general or domain- specific mechanisms? *Cognition, 100*(1), 73–99.

Understanding the Brain – The Birth of a Learning Science, Second Edition. (2007). Organisation for Economic Co-operation and Development - Centre for Educational Research and Innovation (OECD-CERI). Paris, France: Organisation for Economic Co-operation and Development Publication Office. ISBN Number: 9789264029125

Urofsky, M. I. (2020). *The affirmative action puzzle: A living history from reconstruction to today.* Pantheon.

van Batenburg-Eddes, T., & Jolles, J. (2013). How does emotional wellbeing relate to underachievement in a general population sample of young adolescents: a neurocognitive perspective. *Frontiers in psychology, 4,* 673.

van Batenburg-Eddes, T., & Jolles, J. (2013). How does emotional wellbeing relate to underachievement in a general population sample of young adolescents: a neurocognitive perspective. *Frontiers in psychology, 4,* 673.

Van Buuren, M., Wagner, I. C., & Fernández, G. (2019). Functional network interactions at rest underlie individual differences in memory ability. *Learning & Memory, 26*(1), 9–19.

Van Den Heuvel, M. P., Stam, C. J., Kahn, R. S., & Pol, H. E. H. (2009).

Efficiency of functional brain networks and intellectual performance. *Journal of Neuroscience, 29*(23), 7619–7624.

VanTassel-Baska, J. (2005). Gifted programs and services: What are the nonnegotiables? *Theory into practice, 44*(2), 90–97.

van Viersen, S., Kroesbergen, E. H., Slot, E. M., & de Bree, E. H. (2016). High reading skills mask dyslexia in gifted children. *Journal of Learning Disabilities, 49*(2), 189–199.

Verbruggen, F., Notebaert, W., Liefooghe, B., & Vandierendonck, A. (2006). Stimulus-and response-conflict-induced cognitive control in the flanker task. *Psychonomic Bulletin & Review, 13*(2), 328–333.

Verhaeghen, P., Joormann, J., & Aikman, S. N. (2014). Creativity, mood, and the examined life: Self-reflective rumination boosts creativity, brooding breeds dysphoria. *Psychology of Aesthetics, Creativity, and the Arts, 8*(2), 211.

Vining, R. F., McGinley, R. A., Maksvytis, J. J., & Ho, K. Y. (1983). Salivary cortisol: a better measure of adrenal cortical function than serum cortisol. *Annals of clinical biochemistry, 20*(6), 329–335.

Visu-Petra, L., Cheie, L., Benga, O., & Miclea, M. (2011). Cognitive control goes to school: The impact of executive functions on academic performance. *Procedia-Social and Behavioral Sciences, 11*, 240–244.

Vogel, E. K., McCollough, A. W., & Machizawa, M. G. (2005). Neural measures reveal individual differences in controlling access to working memory. *Nature, 438*, 500–503.

Wagner, S. L., Cepeda, I., Krieger, D., Maggi, S., D'Angiulli, A., Weinberg, J., & Grunau, R. E. (2016). Higher cortisol is associated with poorer executive functioning in preschool children: The role of parenting stress, parent coping, and quality of daycare. *Child Neuropsychology, 22*(7), 853–869.

Walcott, C. M., & Landau, S. (2004). The relation between disinhibition and emotion regulation in boys with attention deficit hyperactivity disorder. *Journal of Clinical Child and Adolescent Psychology, 33*(4), 772–782.

Wallace-Wells, D. (2012, Nov 3). A Brain with a Heart. *New York Magazine.* https://nymag.com/news/features/oliver-sacks-2012-11/index.html

Walters, K. L., Mohammed, S. A., Evans-Campbell, T., Beltrán, R. E., Chae, D. H., & Duran, B. (2011). Bodies don't just tell stories, they tell histories:

Embodiment of historical trauma among American Indians and Alaska Natives. *Du Bois Review: Social Science Research on Race, 8*(1), 179–189.

Weir, K. (2018). What makes teams work? *Monitor on Psychology, 49*(8), 46–54.

White, E. J., Hutka, S. A., Williams, L. J., & Moreno, S. (2013). Learning, neural plasticity and sensitive periods: implications for language acquisition, music training and transfer across the lifespan. *Frontiers in systems neuroscience, 7,* 90.

White, P. J., O'Reilly, M., Streusand, W., Levine, A., Sigafoos, J., Lancioni, G., Fragale, C., Pierce,N. & Aguilar, J. (2011). Best practices for teaching joint attention: A systematic review of the intervention literature. *Research in Autism Spectrum Disorders, 5*(4), 1283–1295.

Willoughby, M. T., Blair, C. B., Wirth, R. J., & Greenberg, M. (2012). The measurement of executive function at age 5: Psychometric properties and relationship to academic achievement. *Psychological Assessment, 24*(1), 226.

Wilson, T. D., Reinhard, D. A., Westgate, E. C., Gilbert, D. T., Ellerbeck, N., Hahn, C., Brown, C.L. & Shaked, A. (2014). Just think: The challenges of the disengaged mind. *Science, 345*(6192), 75–77.

Wimmer, H., & Perner, J. (1983). Beliefs about beliefs: Representation and constraining function of wrong beliefs in young children's understanding of deception. *Cognition, 13*(1), 103–128. https://www.thelegacyproject .co.za/2015/04/30/joy-harjo-poet-musician-author/Yerkes, R. M., & Dodson, J. D. (1908). The relation of strength of stimulus to rapidity of habit-formation. *Punishment: Issues and experiments,* 27–41.

Zak, P. (2013). How stories change the brain. *Greater Good: The Science of a Meaningful Life, 17,* 1–4.

Zimmerman, A. W., & Gordon, B. (2001). Neural mechanisms in autism. *The Core Deficit in Autism and Disorders of Relating and Communicating, 5*(1), 119.

Index

About the Author

Layne Kalbfleisch, M.Ed., Ph.D., is the CEO of 2E Consults ® LLC, providing assessment and coaching services. She is a former professor at George Mason University, where she engineered their MRI laboratory and led the Brain, Neuroscience, and Education Special Interest Group of the American Education Research Association from 2011 to 2015. She is a member of the National Science Foundation's (NSF) Group Brain Dynamics In Learning research team and teaches at Northern New Mexico College. Kalbfleisch received the inaugural NSF "Scientist Idol" award for messaging science to the public (2010) and featured on CNN with Dr. Sanjay Gupta, SiriusXM Doctor Radio, and as a columnist for the *Fairfax County Times*. She is Anishinaabe from the Sault Ste. Marie Tribe of the Ojibway.